WHISTLEBLOWING

WHISTLEBLOWING

When It Works—
And Why

Roberta Ann Johnson

LYNNE
RIENNER
PUBLISHERS

BOULDER
LONDON

Published in the United States of America in 2003 by
Lynne Rienner Publishers, Inc.
1800 30th Street, Boulder, Colorado 80301
www.rienner.com

and in the United Kingdom by
Lynne Rienner Publishers, Inc.
3 Henrietta Street, Covent Garden, London WC2E 8LU

Library of Congress Cataloging-in-Publication Data
Johnson, Roberta Ann.
    Whistleblowing : when it works—and why / Roberta Ann Johnson.
    Includes bibliographical references.
    ISBN 1-58826-114-X (alk. paper)
    ISBN 1-58826-139-5 (pb. : alk. paper)
    1. Whistle blowing—United States.   2. Business ethics—United States.   3.
Administrative agencies—Corrupt practices—United States.   4. Whistle blowing—
United States—Case studies.   5. Employees—Dismissal of—United States—Case
studies.   I. Title.
DH60.5.U5 J664   2002
1974'.4—dc21

                                                                          2002073940

British Cataloguing in Publication Data
A Cataloguing in Publication record for this book
is available from the British Library.

Printed and bound in the United States of America

    The paper used in this publication meets the requirements
∞   of the American National Standard for Permanence of
    Paper for Printed Library Materials Z39.48-1984.

    5   4   3

To Robert C. Chope

Confidant, sweetheart, partner, friend

Contents

Preface

On September 11, 2001, foreign terrorists hijacked U.S. planes and flew them into the New York World Trade Center and the Pentagon. In the months that followed, with the United States on high alert, significant numbers of whistleblowers began to come forward with serious concerns about breaches in homeland, air travel, and nuclear security.

During fall 2001, after the Enron corporation was publicly exposed for its misleading and unscrupulous corporate practices, a skyrocketing number of whistleblowers from other publicly traded companies were calling hotlines and e-mailing the Securities and Exchange Commission to report other questionable business practices.

During the rainy California winter months of 2001, the state's energy problems turned into a full-blown crisis. There were rolling blackouts, there was gridlock, and there was plenty of political wrangling. Here too, whistleblowers came forward with valuable information. They said they could demonstrate how the energy problem was not one of scarcity but of company manipulation. Clearly, whistleblowing is part of our lives.

For a dozen years I have read, thought, and learned about whistleblowing. I have attended international ethics conferences, talked to practitioners, and presented and published papers on the topic. My book is the result of those experiences.

During this time, I watched as the number of U.S. whistleblowers grew and the number and kind of whistleblower protections available were expanded and improved. I also watched with fascination as Americans began to encourage whistleblowing in other parts of the world, as an anticorruption tool. By the twenty-first century, whistleblowing was being endorsed, not just by American reformers, but by the U.S. State Department and the U.S. Commerce Department, by the American Bar Association, and by many U.S. multinational businesses. Whistleblowing was no longer a sideshow; it was now part of the main event.

Jeffrey Wigand, "the insider" who blew the whistle on big tobacco, said that the fundamental message of his story was that "an individual can take a stand and make a difference." This is just one of many lessons we can learn from whistleblowers, for the book tells a lot of stories. I also explore the changing social and political environment for whistleblowing, the effectiveness of whistleblower protection, and reasons why only some whistleblowers succeed. What was most challenging was the effort to capture and examine the whistleblower's experience of making the decision itself.

The case studies used in the book were carefully chosen, not because they were average or necessarily representative, but because they were such good vehicles for reinforcing the themes of the chapters. Data for the case studies come from agency documents, congressional hearings and reports, secondary sources such as newspaper accounts, and interviews with major policy actors as well as with ordinary people.

* * *

I am inspired by so many of the people I have interviewed for this project. They have brought purpose and integrity to their life decisions and to their work. They all deserve recognition but there is not enough time or space so I will single out just three very special people from the hundreds I have talked to, to acknowledge and thank—whistleblower Cindy Ossias, attorney in the California Department of Insurance; whistleblower Roger Boisjoly, formerly a Morton Thiokol engineer with NASA; and Tom Devine, the executive director of the Government Accountability Project.

The University of San Francisco has been enormously helpful and supportive of my work in many important ways. They have provided computer tools, research assistants, help from instructional media, and funding for conferences and project-related work and travel. I feel fortunate to be a faculty member at a university where learning and research are so valued and appreciated. Stanley Nel, the dean of Arts and Sciences, has been an especially strong voice for faculty excellence, and he has put his resources on the line in this commitment.

Through the years, many colleagues have contributed to my work on whistleblowing. I especially thank University of Wisconsin, Green Bay, political science and public affairs professor Michael Kraft for his insights, skill, and support. His clarity and understanding of public policy strengthened Chapter 3 considerably. I also wish to thank University of San Francisco professor of philosophy Barbara MacKinnon for her insights and philosophical skills. Her suggestions related to the whistleblower decisionmaking process, analyzed in Chapter 2, were invaluable.

Special thanks go to two USF colleagues in economics, Michael Lehman and Hartmut Fischer, for never letting an article on whistleblowing go by without making me a copy or at least telling me about it. And thanks go to my department colleagues, Brian Weiner and Shalendra Sharma, who have suggested resources that have enriched my work. I am grateful also to University of California, Berkeley, linguistics professor Robin Lakoff for her encouragement and feedback and to Hastings College of Law professor Karen Musalo for her insights about U.S. immigration and naturalization processes.

Suzi Green, our former politics department secretary, already knows that I will be forever grateful to her for her technical help, patience, and computer knowledge. And my student assistants, Aaron Katz, Jodi Higuchi, and Venu Bhakhri, deserve much praise for their intelligence and ingenuity.

The University of San Francisco Law Library assisted me in finding law-related materials and made challenging research often feel effortless. Special thanks go to law school librarians Lee Ryan, John Shafer, and Lille Koski.

On a more personal note, I am grateful to my sister and brother, Nikki Feit and Alan Johnson, for their useful editorial suggestions and to my sister Suellen Johnson for her ideas and encouragement. The saddest acknowledgment of all is for my mother, who always showed enormous interest and enthusiasm for my work, even into her late eighties. She died in April 2001, but she will always remain a part of the project.

Finally, I wish to thank San Francisco State University professor Robert C. Chope, my partner, for his love, help, patience, and support. He offered an eye for style, a shoulder to lean on, an ear for problems, and a hand to hold. He also provided wonderful editorial suggestions and a helpful perspective informed by his own publishing experiences.

—*R. A. J.*

I

The Insider

A l Pacino stood in the rain with only a folded newspaper to shield him from the penetrating downpour. He was portraying the controversial television producer Lowell Bergman in the popular film *The Insider*. Visiting the home of a former tobacco executive, Pacino as Bergman aggressively tried to persuade him to appear on *60 Minutes* as a whistleblower.

But the beleaguered tobacco executive, Jeffrey Wigand (played by Russell Crowe), had signed a nondisclosure agreement and in violating it, he would lose all his company benefits. In the conversation that follows, Bergman captures the kind of choice the whistleblower faces.

> Bergman: Why are you working for tobacco in the first place?
> Wigand: I can't talk about it. The work I was supposed to do might have had some positive effect. I don't know. It could have been beneficial. Mostly, I got paid a lot. I took the money. My wife was happy. My kids had good medical, good schools. I got a great house. I mean, what the hell's wrong with that?
> Bergman: Nothing's wrong with that. That's it. You're making money. You're providing for your family. What could be wrong with that?
> Wigand: I always thought of myself as a man of science, that's what's wrong with it.
> Bergman: Then, you're in a state of conflict, Jeff. Because here's how it lays out—if you got vital insider stuff that the citizens of the United States, for their welfare, really do need to know, and you feel impelled to disclose it and violate your agreement in doing so that's one thing. On the other hand, if you want to honor this agreement then that's simple. You say nothing. You do nothing. There's only one guy who can figure that out for you, and that's you, all by yourself.

Wigand decided. He came forward as a whistleblower and the drama of this story was captured on film.

Jeffrey Wigand had worked for the Brown and Williamson Tobacco Corporation (B&W) for four years. From 1989 to 1993, he was vice president of research and development, in charge of hundreds of scientists and workers, with an annual salary of about $400,000. Wigand, who had a Ph.D. in biochemistry and endocrinology from the University of Buffalo, had been frustrated by B&W when he attempted to develop a "safer" cigarette, one with lower carcinogens (Miethe 1999: 200–201). Wigand also experienced the company's stunning resistance to his recommendations for changing and removing cancer-causing tobacco additives and flavoring from their cigarettes. After he confronted the CEO on these health-related matters, Wigand was unceremoniously fired.

In 1994, Wigand became a whistleblower. Among his many allegations (Miethe 1999: 202), Jeffrey Wigand accused B&W of using additives to manipulate nicotine delivery, of editing out incriminating data from company reports, of intentionally misleading the public about tobacco's addictive qualities, and of other serious wrongdoing. He exposed the company's questionable practices, first with the Food and Drug Administration in the spring of 1994, and then with the U.S. Department of Justice, which was investigating the industry's efforts to make a "fire-safe cigarette."

Wigand testified as an expert witness in other cases, as well. Among these were a civil action lawsuit in Massachusetts, a libel suit in Virginia, and legal action filed against tobacco companies by the attorneys general of forty states seeking reimbursement for illnesses caused by smoking; the case was settled June 20, 1997 (Miethe 1999: 202; Rubin 2000).

Dr. Wigand's insider testimony against the tobacco industry appeared in court documents, newspapers, and on television. The company retaliated against him with lawsuits and negative publicity. Wigand accused them of retaliating with physical threats.

How did this story find its way onto the CBS-TV show *60 Minutes*, the most watched news program in the United States? How did it become the theme of a Hollywood movie? A lot was determined by Lowell Bergman.

Lowell Bergman produced *60 Minutes*. Since the program's inception in September 1968, nearly every *60 Minutes* has featured someone exposing unethical, dangerous, or corrupt activity. In fact, the program receives hundreds of solicitations each week from people wanting to be on to expose wrongdoing (Tedesco 2001).

Jeffrey Wigand had already been quoted on television and in newspapers, and had testified in court. Nevertheless, his appearing on *60 Minutes* represented a giant leap toward connecting with the public. At the peak of network television, in the late 1970s, *60 Minutes* had 30–40 million viewers. Even with the competition of cable television, at the time the Wigand program aired, it still reached a respectable 18 million (Tedesco 2001).

According to Lowell Bergman, it was "a fluke" that the movie *The Insider* got made at all. In the beginning of 1996, it wasn't clear that the Wigand story would ever be aired on *60 Minutes*. Bergman was close to the point of leaving CBS and he started "talking to people in Hollywood." Michael Mann, a Hollywood producer of such projects as *Crime Story* and *Miami Vice*, had been following the Wigand story at *60 Minutes*. Over the years, Bergman had brought him ideas he thought would make good movies, but they were always rejected. In January 1996, when Bergman told Mann it was "over for him at *60 Minutes*," Mann said, "I think you got the movie." "What is it?" asked Bergman. Mann answered, "It's you." He was serious and he was the reason "the movie happened" (Bergman 2000).

Jeffrey Wigand thought the picture accurately reflected the truth. He was flattered that Russell Crowe invested so much time and effort in his portrayal. "He does an exquisite job of portraying someone who is alive. It's uncanny. He's like a clone. There is a tremendous amount of accuracy and precision in replicating the feelings, the emotions, the psychological drama, the gait. He said he wanted to do me honor" (Rubin 2000).

For Bergman, it was only through Hollywood that the story was able to reach the movie-going audience. The filmmaker's assumption, of course, was that *The Insider* would reach a sympathetic audience, an audience who might identify with, rather than condemn, whistleblowing. They were right. During the last three decades, whistleblowing had become a prominent part of U.S. vocabulary, culture, and organizational life. In fact, citizens in the United States blow the whistle on waste, fraud, and abuse more than anywhere else in the world.

Definition and History

Whistleblowing is a distinct form of dissent (Elliston et al. 1985: 3–15). There is an agreed-upon definition that has four component parts: (1) An individual acts with the intention of making information public;

(2) the information is conveyed to parties outside the organization who make it public and a part of the public record; (3) the information has to do with possible or actual nontrivial wrongdoing in an organization[1]; and (4) the person exposing the agency is not a journalist or ordinary citizen, but a member or former member of the organization.

While there is general agreement as to who can be called a whistle-blower, the term *whistleblower* used in this way has unclear origins. Miceli and Near believe that the whistleblower analogy "is to an official on a playing field, such as a football referee, who can blow the whistle to stop action" (1992: 15). Others have suggested that the term *blowing the whistle* derives from the caricature of the "bulbous-cheeked English Bobby wheezing away on his whistle when the maiden cries 'stop thief'" (Branch 1979: 237).

Although the connection with games and cartoons may seem to give the word *whistleblower* a somewhat flippant feel, the term was used in a serious way starting in the 1960s to distinguish this set of "dissenters" or "inside informants" from informants who provided evidence against the Mafia, or former communists who "named names" for the FBI and assorted congressional committees (Glazer and Glazer 1988: 56). Activist and author David Bollier credits a conference organized by Ralph Nader in 1971 as having legitimized the use of the term for insiders who expose scandal (Bollier 2002).[2]

Since the early 1970s, whistleblowing has become a common means of describing dissent in a bureaucracy, particularly when issues of public health, safety, fraud, or abuse of office are involved. The United States has successfully exported the idea to the rest of the world, as we shall see in Chapter 6.

It is clear that for Americans, whistleblowing is a part of the cultural landscape. Whistleblowing has been a theme in Hollywood films such as *Serpico*, *Silkwood*, *Marie*, and of course *The Insider*.[3] In addition, whistleblowers are often featured as heroes and experts on news shows. Currently, the most significant pattern related to whistleblowing is that it is on the increase.

So why are there so many whistleblowers in the United States? Five factors help to explain this phenomenon: (1) changes in the bureaucracy itself, (2) the wide range of laws that encourage whistle-blowing, (3) the federal and state whistleblower protections, (4) institutional support for whistleblowers, and (5) a culture that often values whistleblowing.

Changing Bureaucracy

It is likely that changes within the bureaucracies themselves account for some of the increases in whistleblowing. One important change is in the job qualifications of bureaucrats. Whistleblowing seems to have been stimulated by the increasing educational level and professional training of public officials. Wakefield suggests that we are entering the age of the "specialist, expert, and technocrat"(1976: 663). Specially trained experts may feel that they have a distinct perspective on public problems and solutions, one that may be nonnegotiable. As one whistleblower confided, "Being trained as a scientist rather than a politician, I have never found negotiations to be a particularly satisfactory means of solving problems" (Pearson, cited in Frome 1978: 51). Hence, some professionals may be less prone than other officials to compromise when it comes to questionable decisionmaking or wrongdoing.[4]

Over the past several decades, the federal government has employed significantly larger numbers of scientists, engineers, and other professionals, partly to staff new or greatly expanded health, safety, and environmental programs in agencies such as the Environmental Protection Agency (EPA). A disproportionately high number of professionals engage in whistleblowing (Parmerlee, Near, and Jensen 1982), and Elliston et al. hypothesize that the activity is likely to occur when "higher standards are expected of professionals" (1985: 167). Professional employees may be required and may feel obliged to follow their professional codes of ethics (Westman 1991: 28).

Old organizations taking on new responsibilities may also induce whistleblowing. Elliston et al. identify organizational structures themselves as stimuli to whistleblowing. Whistleblowing, they say, is more likely to occur "when organizations rigidly conform to past practices rather than adopt new practices more suitable to their changed environments" (1985: 44). Wakefield also describes the "complex of new decisions which do not substitute for older decisions but are net additions." This complex of new decisions adds to the bureaucrat's repertoire of responsibility in new areas where rules are less certain; the uncertainty of rules can make whistleblowing more likely.

Elliston et al. explain the new uncertainty in a similar fashion. Whistleblowing is more likely to occur, they say, in organizations with "more technologically complex tasks," and "new scientific and complex technologies and developments." In such cases, there is likely to be more uncertainty about the proper course of action to promote the public's interest (1985: 166), and also a greater prevalence of professionals who may disagree with the organization's decision.

Laws Encourage Whistleblowing

In the United States, whistleblowing is also encouraged by statute as an ethical duty. According to the Ethics in Government Act of 1978, as amended, and under the 1990 Executive Order 12731, federal agencies are required to provide ethics orientation to all federal employees. At these annual training sessions, employees are notified that they are required to disclose waste, fraud, and abuse to appropriate authorities.

In addition, in 1980, a Code of Ethics for Government Service (PL 96-303) was unanimously passed by Congress and was signed into law by President Ronald Reagan. It requires persons in government service to "put loyalty to the highest moral principles above loyalty to persons, party, or Government department" (Senate Antitrust Subcommittee of the Committee on the Judiciary 1983).

Furthermore, the creation of agency hotlines make it even easier for potential whistleblowers to act. In the early 1980s, consistent with the Ethics Code, federal hotlines were established in each federal agency to encourage whistleblowers to report government waste and fraud. For years, the Department of Defense (DoD) whistleblower hotline alone has received over a thousand whistleblower calls per month (Department of Defense Inspector General 1992: 4-1). Those using the hotline reflect a great variety of motivations and disclosures; there is no typical case. The following two experiences with the DoD hotline tell interesting stories about whistleblower tenacity and luck as well as hotline promise and limitations.

Tom Reay

Tom Reay was stationed on the USS *Fulton*, a submarine tender (repair ship). In 1986, he was in charge of the Division for Electronic Repairs. After four months, he began to notice that naval personnel were being "ripped off" on the price of parts. He began to go to "outside sources" to buy the pieces he needed. He kept a list of all the parts and their prices and his division began to save a lot of money.

About this time, he said, someone gave him the 800 DoD hotline number and every Friday he would call with a list of two to five items he had purchased at a savings. It was done with such regularity that he began joking with the hotline operator, whom he got to know by name. He started calling the hotline in November 1986.

Reay's executive officer asked him what he was doing that was saving them money and then permitted him to continue. Others warned him that he "better watch out." His response, since he was not a career seaman, was "What will they do—kick me out?"

Reay left the navy in late 1987. In November 1988 a package from the navy was delivered to him and, at that moment, he admitted that he feared the worst—punishment for his initiative and his whistleblowing. Instead, the package contained a $500 award for his "light bulb suggestion." It seems that a navy contractor had been charging $18 for the tiny light bulbs used on control indicators. They burned out frequently and many needed to be purchased. Tom Reay had gone to Radio Shack and bought them for 15 cents each (Reay 1990).

Nancy Kusen

Nancy Kusen brought a much more complicated situation to the DoD hotline. She was an administrative contracting officer with the Defense Logistics Agency, Defense Contract Administration Services Management Area (DCASMA) in Pittsburgh, Pennsylvania. She had been working for the Department of Defense for over a decade when she tried to blow the whistle on agency wrongdoing.

For one year (1984–1985), Kusen reported to DCASMA management about suspected contract irregularities with Elliot Company, a subsidiary of United Technologies Corporation. DCASMA managers refused to recognize and correct the irregularities. The DoD Pittsburgh office of the Defense Criminal Investigative Service, whom she contacted, also chose not to intervene. For three and a half more years, Kusen tried to get the suspected wrongdoing addressed.

From June 1986 through March 1987, Kusen sent twenty-six letters to the DoD hotline. Twenty-four of her letters contained specific supporting documentation attached to them, including audit reports, progress payment requests, government contractor correspondence, and copies of contracts. Her allegations included fraud, collusion, overcharging, duplicate charging, and defective and substandard workmanship. What was at stake was an estimated 6–7 million recoverable dollars.

Ironically, when the hotline accepted her case, they referred it back directly for investigation to the same Pittsburgh office and special agent whose lack of investigation caused Kusen to turn to the hotline in the first place. A year later, the hotline investigators found her case not substantiated, and it was closed.

Articles about the abuses did appear in Pittsburgh newspapers, but they were not enough to make Kusen successful in her claim, and when she tried writing directly to Rear Admiral M. E. Chang, Office of the Naval Inspector General, the response she got was a dismissive, "Kusen, give up already." Meanwhile, Kusen experienced lowered performance appraisals and a denial of promotion.

Kusen's claims were finally validated, not by a hotline investigation, newspaper reporters, or the inspector general. Rather she was vindicated by an analysis of an independent group, the U.S. Navy Price Fighter Detachment, which conducted an independent "should cost" analysis. It compared what the Elliot delivery order for twenty-six rotor assemblies cost the government and what they "should have cost" the government. The overcharge for just one delivery order was a whopping $133,317.60. The independent group's report was definitive and changed the outcome of the Kusen controversy.

Kusen's story ended happily for her. Four DoD managers, guilty of whistleblower reprisals against Kusen, were removed; Kusen received monetary and sustained superior performance awards and she was promoted to administrative contracting officer. Interestingly, with her promotion, she was made Elliot Company's new contracting officer (Kusen 1989).

As the experiences of Tom Reay and Nancy Kusen illustrate, whistleblower hotlines are an important feature of the U.S. bureaucracy. Hotline use was further reinforced in the administration of Bill Clinton and Al Gore by their March 1993 much-publicized "National Performance Review," which invited all citizens to call a hotline number to report bureaucratic waste. This call for a "national performance review" resulted in over 30,000 responses, most sent or phoned in during President Clinton's early months in office. Clearly, U.S. citizens were not afraid to use hotlines to blow the whistle on alleged or suspected wrongdoing.

In addition to laws that establish codes of ethics and hotlines, there are other laws that encourage U.S. whistleblowers. Under the Federal False Claims Act, some whistleblowers can be awarded 15–25 percent of the money their whistleblowing recovers for a federal agency. That certainly motivates some whistleblowers.

"To say I never thought about financial rewards is absurd," said whistleblower Pat Shull, who received $25 million as a result of exposing wrongdoing by the Bank of America in 1998 (Zuckerman 1998). The *San Francisco Chronicle* boldly announced, "Blowing the whistle on those who rip off the government has become a big business." In 1996 alone, 360 whistleblower cases were filed with the U.S. Justice Department alleging fraud against the federal government. In fact, over an eleven-year period, the Department of Justice recovered more than $1.8 billion in 225 cases; the whistleblowers involved collected $200 million (Sinton 1997: E-1).

Laws Also Protect

Whistleblowers are also encouraged by federal and state laws that promise protection against retaliation. A wave of laws containing such employee protections were passed, beginning in the 1960s. During this decade, and those to follow, government efforts regulating business brought with them an expectation that employees would help in enforcing the new laws in areas such as environmental protection, public health and safety, and civil rights. Embodied in these regulations were various provisions protecting employees against retaliation (Westman 1991: 8).

Currently, the wide range of federal laws with such provisions include the Uniform Health and Safety Whistleblower Protection Act, the Occupational Safety and Health Act, the Savings and Loan whistleblower statute, the Toxic Substance Act, Superfund, and laws regulating mine safety, clean air, and clean water. In addition to these, there is also the important 1978 Whistleblower Protection Act. It was revised and strengthened in 1989 and in 1994, and will be discussed at length in Chapter 5, along with the other pertinent federal and state laws.

Individual states have joined in as well. By 1990, "twenty states . . . had statutes that protect public-sector employees from discharge in retaliation for reporting their employer's unlawful conduct and ten states had enacted statutes protecting whistleblowing in both the public and the private sectors. By 1999, nearly all states provided some form of whistleblower protection and nearly all states had statutes protecting employees who reported violations of state and federal laws or regulations" (Egan 1990: 416–417; Miethe 1999: 108).

Support from Organizations and Institutions

News media, Congress, and helpful organizations all encourage U.S. whistleblowing. The example of Jeffrey Wigand illustrates not only how whistleblowers can be turned into heroes, but also how the media can contribute to this. According to James Q. Wilson, "The emergence of a new generation of reporters with a more adversarial stance toward government" has made journalists more attentive to whistleblowers (1989: 88).

Newspapers and television unfailingly assist whistleblowers. They tell their stories; they engage the public; they publicize and sustain interest in the alleged wrongdoing. Television and the popular press nationalize, popularize, and sometimes personalize a whistleblower story. Whistleblowers *need* media coverage.

Michael D'Antonio, in *Atomic Harvest* (1993), describes the important support the media has given to whistleblowers who exposed dangerous conditions at nuclear weapons facilities. He demonstrates with the case of whistleblower Casey Ruud, at the Hanford nuclear installation. In this case, Ruud turned to Eric Nadler, a *Seattle Times* reporter, to expose serious problems. Following a congressional investigation, "the entire industry was shut down," with the help of reporter Keith Schneider of the *New York Times*.

Media coverage allows whistleblowers to establish their credibility and legitimacy for their cause while stimulating public interest. As already described, the television news magazine show *60 Minutes* has often used whistleblowers because of the program's muckraking format.

However, Nancy Kusen's case also illustrates how media coverage, while very important for the whistleblower, does not guarantee a positive outcome. Although Kusen's allegations were described in the sustained reporting of Pittsburgh newspapers, she needed other support to make her case.

In addition to extensive media coverage there are two institutional factors unique to the United States that help explain the country's significant and growing number of whistleblowers. These two contributing ingredients are: (1) the system of divided government (checks and balances), and (2) the American propensity to form organizations.

Checks and Balances

In terms of institutional arrangements, the whistleblower benefits from the unique system of divided government in the United States. The U.S.

nonparliamentary system separates the legislative body from the executive branch to create constitutional "checks and balances." The executive and legislative branches are real institutional rivals and adversaries. This is even more so when the two branches are of different political parties.

An important way the legislative branch can flex its muscles vis-à-vis the executive branch is through congressional oversight of the executive agencies. Whistleblowers who come forward with insider information are their star witnesses. Congress holds public hearings, getting testimony on inefficiency, illegalities, abuse, and wrongdoing from whistleblowers. The information and the publicity they provide gives the legislature entrée into what the agency does and can be harnessed to legislative ends. It is no surprise that, regardless of what political party controls Congress, whistleblower protection legislation is always unanimously passed. It serves the interest of the legislature because Congress can elevate, legitimize, and publicize whistleblowers and their concerns and, at the same time, forward their own.

Congress has enhanced its right to know while protecting their whistleblowers. In 1988, Congress passed two federal statutes, one that protects witnesses in congressional investigations from intimidation (18 U.S.C. 1505) and another that specifically guarantees federal employees the right to provide congressional members with information (5 U.S.C. 7211).

In 1989, with the help of Representatives Patricia Schroeder and William Coyne, whistleblower Nancy Kusen gave testimony at a congressional hearing for a House subcommittee whose focus was hotlines and whistleblower protection. After years of frustration, speaking in this public forum allowed Kusen to reestablish her credibility while the visibility probably helped protect her from further reprisals.

This was also the case with Jennifer Long, who was "the star witness at the 1997 hearings before the Senate Finance Committee that examined alleged abuses by the IRS." As an auditor with the IRS, she testified in Congress that her agency "harassed" taxpayers (Associated Press 2001: A-8). Long was the only IRS whistleblower who did not use a protective screen or disguise her voice to conceal her identity. Her testimony was given in nationally televised hearings.

In 1999, following Long's public insider testimony, the IRS tried to fire her, and in 2001 they tried to block her being licensed by the Texas Board of Public Accountancy. But each time she was targeted by her agency, she was protected from their retaliatory action by an inquiry or a well-publicized letter to the IRS commissioner from a member of Congress (Associated Press 2001: A-8).[5]

Congress has instituted specific agency reporting requirements related to whistleblowing. In 1978, with the passage of the Inspectors General Act, Congress not only mandated executive agencies to establish hotlines, it also required each agency's Office of the Inspector General (IG) to produce a "Semiannual Report to the Congress," which included a discussion of agency whistleblower activities and protections. The IG reports from the Department of Defense, for example, even included illustrations of substantiated whistleblower reprisal cases.

Organizations

In addition to the news media and Congress, an important third factor contributing to the country's unique institutional context for whistleblowers relates to Americans' propensity to form groups. Today, nongovernment whistleblower organizations abound. They encourage, support, and sometimes even fund whistleblower efforts and help make the whistleblower feel less isolated and more empowered.

As we have seen, the Nancy Kusen case was made and saved by a nongovernment group, the U.S. Navy Price Fighter Detachment. Their independent analysis, which revealed significant discrepancies and blatant overpricing, proved the pattern of overcharging that Kusen had alleged. This nonprofit organization, like hundreds of others, helps and serves whistleblowers.

Other organizations have been created whose focus is on the work of particular agencies. For example, the nonprofit organization Forest Service Employees for Environmental Ethics, based in Eugene, Oregon, has a membership primarily of former employees of the Forest Service. They encourage whistleblowers and they act as a watchdog for the agency. In addition, the group Public Employees for Environmental Responsibility (PEER), which has state chapters made up of federal agents in various states, provides whistleblower support for Department of the Interior and Army Corps of Engineers employees. Another example is the National Association of Treasury Agents, which acts as a support base for Treasury Department whistleblowers.

Some professional organizations have focused on whistleblowing. The Tucson-based Arizona chapter of the American Association of

University Professors (AAUP) has, in fact, made reform of whistle-blower protection its major goal and has assisted in protecting the careers of a number of university whistleblowers.

Another professional organization involved in aiding whistleblowers is the American Association for the Advancement of Science (AAAS). AAAS has used its prestige to lobby for increased whistleblower protection and has assisted scientists who were fired or disciplined for exposing violations of federal environmental regulations. Whistleblowers have also been recipients of the AAAS Scientific Freedom and Responsibility Award.

Some organizations, and even some individuals, have offered financial support to whistleblowers. The *PA Times*, a public administration newsletter, announced in their June 1989 issue that an endowment fund had been created by an individual that would award $10,000 to three whistleblowers per year (McCormick 1989: 3).

Many groups specialize in particular services. Taxpayers Against Fraud, established in 1986 and based in Washington, D.C., specializes in and has been extremely successful in helping individuals pursue False Claims Act lawsuits. Since 1981, the nonprofit organization Project on Government Oversight (POGO, formerly the Project on Military Procurement), also in Washington, D.C., has provided emotional support and sometimes independent investigations for government whistleblowers whose cases are not widely publicized. Finally, Integrity International, created by psychologist Don Soekin, has provided psychological support and needed coaching on due-process requirements for dozens of whistleblowers.

In the mid-1990s, the National Whistleblower Center emerged. A Washington, D.C.–based nonprofit organization, it offered information and services that included training seminars on whistleblower laws; CD-ROMs on the latest court decisions on whistleblowing; a whistleblower litigation handbook on environmental, health, and safety claims; and an attorney referral service and help line. Their quarterly newsletter was first published in winter 1994. In addition to nuclear and medical areas, they specialize in FBI whistleblowing.

The Government Accountability Project (GAP) is the most impressive whistleblower organization because of its long track record and its participation as a witness in congressional hearings and as an expert in General Accounting Office reports. GAP is the premier whistleblower organization in the United States. In fact, GAP "alumni" have spun off to form other organizations, and as we will see in Chapter 6, GAP is in the process of educating and training about whistleblowing around the world.

GAP was created in 1977. Its purpose was to hold the federal government accountable by assisting whistleblowers who challenge policies and practices that threatened public health and safety and the environment (Government Accountability Project 1989b: 1; Clark 1988: 1). They pursue their mission in the United States through counseling, by offering legal expertise, by conducting investigations to help expose cover-ups, by working to strengthen whistleblower laws, and by disseminating information and publishing scholarly articles (Devine and Morales 2001).

GAP's annual budget is close to $1.5 million, and through the years it has helped hundreds of whistleblowers with legal assistance. There are many things that illustrate GAP's success and level of integration into mainstream political activities. The most impressive, perhaps, is that GAP is considered an expert by government agencies such as the General Accounting Office (GAO), by members of Congress who use GAP testimony about whistleblowing in their reports, and by the U.S. State Department, which has sent GAP personnel to other countries to publicly advocate for whistleblowing. In addition, GAP has been a reputable source of information for newspapers such as the *Wall Street Journal*. Even actor Robert Redford has expressed his support and is quoted in some of their solicitation letters sent to potential donors.

Cultural Values

The shift in cultural values provides, perhaps, the most important explanation for the large increase in numbers of whistleblowers in the United States. Over the last few decades, U.S. attitudes toward whistleblowing and whistleblowers have changed. Loyalty to team and group has always been valued in the American culture, not only on the children's playground but also in corporate boardrooms and public agencies. Some have argued that loyalty is especially important in a government agency because "the disloyal employee can hurt the collective interest of the organization by damaging its *image*, the public face on which an appropriation usually depends" (Branch 1979: 232).[6]

As the number of whistleblowers has increased (U.S. Merit Systems Protection Board 1993: 9) and as government and media

"I'm only a finger-pointer now, but someday I'll be a whistle-blower."

reports about them have also increased, the public's attitude toward whistleblowing appears to have grown more supportive. Even mainstream cartoons are positive about whistleblowing and while the exposed agencies may continue to characterize whistleblowers as disloyal (or worse), media coverage and congressional attention often present the same whistleblowers as heroes. As we have seen, whistleblower Jeffrey Wigand was popularly portrayed as a hero to the public although he was clearly viewed as a traitor in the tobacco industry.

A strong belief in individualism is part of the American personality (Patterson 1998: 4; Ketab 1992). The public's receptivity to whistleblowing is supported by this long-held belief. As Robert G. Vaughn observes, "Whistleblowing is a highly individual undertaking even when several employees are engaged in it; it relies on personal decisions about its propriety and a willingness to accept the risks attendant to it" (1999: 587).

This connection to the traditional American value of individualism may be especially stimulated by popular press coverage and academic studies of whistleblowing, which often emphasize the personal suffering and isolation the whistleblowers experience because of their courageous exposure of wrongdoing (Nader, Petkas, and Blackwell 1972; Glazer and Glazer 1989; Frome 1978; Branch 1979; Weisband and Frank 1975; Senate 1983). Whistleblowers themselves relate and connect to the value of individualism. For example, Jeffrey Wigand believed that the fundamental message of his story was that "an individual can take a stand and make a difference" (Rubin 2000).

The U.S. public is also able to see whistleblowers in a positive light and as heroes because of a general cynicism and a lack of trust in government. Goodsell has described these feelings (1994) and they have increased steadily since the late 1960s (Patterson 1998). Glazer and Glazer point to "public disillusionment," "cynicism," and "skepticism" (1988: 57), and Louis Harris even called this lack of trust in government a "full-blown crisis of confidence" (Cooper 1979: 77). The American public's more recent less cynical attitude, reflected in surveys conducted post–September 11, 2001, is very likely just temporary.[7]

There is a third factor contributing to the public's more positive spin on whistleblowing. Whistleblowers increasingly are raising health and safety issues that people personally care about. This also helps explain the public's receptivity toward whistleblowing. Elliston et al. suggest, for example, that whistleblowing is "more likely to occur when there is increasing public concern for environmental, health, and safety problems" (1985: 167) and when there is concern for the government's effectiveness in monitoring hazards and maintaining safety standards (Glazer and Glazer 1988: 57).

Allegations of an unsafe nuclear power plant, unsafe food or water, insufficient protection from pollutants, or unsafe aviation practices are problem areas that are of great interest to much of the general public. Exposing danger, abuse, inefficiency, or wasteful spending in these areas, even by a whistleblower, might be appreciated as a kind of public service.

This was the case in the following example where a small community turned a local whistleblower into a hero.

Aaron Ahearn

Aaron Ahearn became a whistleblower. He was a sailor who served on the USS *Abraham Lincoln*. Originally from Santa Cruz, California, he blew the whistle on the ship's excessive polluting.

The USS *Abraham Lincoln* is the world's largest carrier. It generates a half a ton of plastic trash each day. Whistleblower Ahearn exposed the ship's practices of throwing the plastic garbage overboard and of discharging raw sewage closer to shore than the allowable three nautical miles. In an effort to change policy, he complained to his supervisors and confided in the ship's chaplain, but to no avail. When he became a whistleblower and went AWOL to protest the ship's practice, his story was picked up by CBS news. Ahearn's position was simple: "I grew up surfing in Santa Cruz and was taught not to pollute."

The Santa Cruz community made him their hero. A San Francisco weekly newspaper reported that "after the ecology-minded surfer from Santa Cruz went AWOL in February, he received a hero's welcome in his hometown where fundraisers were held in his honor and the Board of Supervisors passed a resolution supporting him" (*San Francisco Weekly* 1993).

Scandal and Catastrophe

Scandal and catastrophe have hurried the public's acceptance of whistleblowing. The 1986 space shuttle *Challenger* disaster, which will be more fully discussed in Chapter 2, has been called a "milestone event for whistleblowing" because it stimulated a groundswell of public support and public interest in whistleblower protection reform (Clark 2002).

According to Louis Clark, executive director of the Government Accountability Project, the demotion of three Morton Thiokol engineers because of their whistleblowing testimony to an investigating government commission (the Rogers Commission) caused Congress to "get the message." The public was alarmed, grieved the *Challenger* tragedy, and supported the whistleblowers. "As a response to their constituents," Clark said, "Congress flipped into an interest in whistleblower protection," and soon after they revised and strengthened whistleblower laws. The resulting congressional reforms, passed in 1988 and 1989, are described in Chapter 5.

More recently, the Enron collapse and scandal in 2001, with fallout continuing into 2002, also stimulated public interest and support of whistleblowing (Chaddock 2002; Mayer and Joyce 2002). Enron's questionable corporate practices were front-page news and so were reports of public disillusionment and skepticism about corporate behavior (Fineman and Isikoff 2002; Stephens 2002; Graf and Orr 2002; Bayon 2002; Schmidt and Behr 2002; Yardley 2002; Pender 2002; Oppel 2002). Emerging from the mess and making front-page news herself was Enron vice president Sherron S. Watkins, who was characterized as a lone whistleblower,[8] and whose testimony was the centerpiece of well-publicized congressional hearings (Nusbaum 2002; *New York Times* 2002; Lochhead 2002; Dowd 2002; Abramson 2002).

Public outrage and constituent anger over Enron stimulated many members of Congress to begin to consider seriously whistleblower protection legislation for employees of publicly traded companies (Senate 2002: S1785) and to consider legislation—aptly referred to as the "Paul Revere Freedom to Warn" act (Clark 2002; Chadock 2002)—that provided a jury trial in federal district court for government and private-sector whistleblowers who are harassed for going to Congress with information, (Government Accountability Project 2002a: 7). The scandal also stimulated a skyrocketing number of whistleblower complaints, including a dramatic rise in complaints to the Securities and Exchange Commission (Fairbanks 2002).

By April 2002, "two of the nation's largest firms that maintain hotlines for other companies" (Pinkerton and Network) were reporting "a noticeable increase in employee calls." Since the Enron scandal, Pinkerton Consulting and Investigations, a company responsible for

"You know how to whistle, don't you? Just pick up
the phone and call the S.E.C."

maintaining hotlines for approximately 1,000 companies, reported a 12 percent rise in calls; Network Inc., which maintains toll-free hotlines for approximately 650 companies, reported that their calls were up 35 percent (Mayer and Joyce 2002: H-4).

Post–September 11

Public safety has always been an important motivator. In the early 1990s, federal employees were surveyed on the factors that might cause them to report illegal or wasteful activities. Fully 96 percent of the 13,000 respondents labeled as "very important" activities that might endanger people's lives (U.S. Merit Systems Protection Board 1993: 10). However, while concern with public health and safety has always been a strong motivator for whistleblowers, it is an even stronger factor in the aftermath of September 11, 2001. The marked increase in whistleblowing following the September attacks may reflect the addition of a new ingredient—a sense of patriotic duty (Morrison 2001).

Following September 11, GAP's whistleblower intake calls tripled. Growing numbers of whistleblowers were concerned about homeland, aviation, and nuclear security. For example, a Federal Aviation Administration official alleged bureaucratic negligence and security breaches at airports around the country; a former Customs special agent expressed concern over inadequate inspection and border security related to railcars; and an expert at the Department of Energy reported concerns about safeguards against attacks at nuclear weapons facilities.

These and other cases were being treated seriously by the public, by members of Congress, and by the press. By December 2001, the Office of Special Counsel (OSC) had opened four investigations of alleged retaliation against federal employees who had voiced national-security concerns. Such a quick response by OSC "often indicates the case has merit" (Morrison 2001: 1; Government Accountability Project 2002b).

Tying It All Together

In the United States, people blow the whistle on waste, fraud, and abuse more than anywhere else in the world. It was in the United States, after all, that the term *whistleblowing* itself was coined. This chapter has explored the cultural and institutional factors that help account for the large number of U.S. whistleblowers.

Of course, there is whistleblower protective legislation and there is mandated government ethics training, which encourages employees to expose wrongdoing. But other countries have protective legislation with nowhere near the numbers of whistleblowers, and besides, as we will see in Chapter 5, studies of whistleblower protection suggest that the protection offered is far from perfect.

U.S. whistleblowers may be encouraged to act by the promise of financial gain. The Federal False Claims Act promises the whistleblower 15–25 percent of the money their agency recovers because of their whistleblowing. However, this law only accounts for a fraction of U.S. whistleblower cases and a large government study suggests that it is not a major motivator (U.S. Merit Systems Protection Board 1993: 10). Thus, financial gain is not as important as other uniquely American institutional and cultural factors in explaining the whistleblower phenomenon. Clearly the most important factor is the United States' changing attitude toward whistleblowing.

The U.S. public seems to have shifted to a more positive point of view about whistleblowing. This has been due, in part, to the increase and positive spin of media coverage. Newspapers, magazines, and television news shows often report about whistleblowing and feature whistleblowers as public-interest heroes. The positive spin the media gives to the individual whistleblower is likely to resonate with the general belief in "individualism" and a general distrust of government, helping connect U.S. citizens to the whistleblower experience.

In addition, whistleblowers who are credited with exposing dangers or health hazards are often seen as performing a public service. Thus, during the last three decades, whistleblower stories have become more numerous and are viewed more positively. Today, the U.S. public is more sympathetic to whistleblowing.

Changes within the bureaucracy itself also help stimulate whistleblowing. Government bureaucrats are increasingly better educated and trained. Many are scientists, engineers, and other professionals, and it is the government workers who are professionals who are more likely to be engaged in whistleblowing. In addition, older bureaucratic organizations are involved in expanding government activities and some newer government agencies are involved in public health and safety. Expanding into new areas, the bureaucratic "rules of the game" may be less certain and the health and safety stakes may be higher. This combination is likely to encourage whistleblowing.

Two other factors—institutional checks and balances and the exis-

tence of large numbers of support groups—also contribute to the large
and growing number of U.S. whistleblowers. These factors are unique
to the United States but are rarely credited for contributing to whistleblowing.

Constitutional checks and balances include congressional oversight
authority over the executive branch. In the process of pursuing their
oversight role, Congress has gratefully received documents from
whistleblowers that would not normally be available to them. Congress
needs whistleblowers. More and more, Congress has become responsible for aiding and protecting whistleblowers and giving them credibility
and a platform. It is no surprise that regardless of party or ideology,
Congress always passes whistleblower protective legislation unanimously.

The United States' unique propensity to form groups also significantly contributes to whistleblowing. Whistleblowers can tap into a network that offers professional, financial, psychological, legal, and technical help from hundreds of groups available to offer advice and
support. This means that, unlike whistleblowers in most other countries,
U.S. whistleblowers are not alone. A ready network of assistance and
support may also help create a climate that encourages whistleblowing
activity.

Further, agency hotlines, another distinctly U.S. innovation, appear
to stimulate whistleblowing. This occurs regardless of their many deficiencies, including the fact that large numbers of government employees either do not know about their agencies' hotlines or if they know
about them, do not trust their safety. In fact, as the Kusen case demonstrates, and as we will see in Chapter 5, hotline investigations have
surely been imperfect at fully protecting whistleblowers and have often
been sorely inadequate in getting to the truth. Nevertheless, record
numbers of government employees continue to contact hotlines each
month and federal agencies regularly claim large savings because of
these hotline calls.

It appears that, however inadequate and unfair hotlines may be, just
the fact of their existence, the activities that surround them, and the
scrutiny the hotlines get from Congress and other government and nongovernment agencies contribute to an environment that encourages
whistleblowing.

Finally, the tragedy of September 11, 2001, and the scandal and collapse of Enron, WorldCom, Global Crossing, and the like, have created
an atmosphere even more conducive to, and supportive of, whistleblow-

ing. The calamity and scandal have shaken the economy and have caused the U.S. citizenry to be on high alert. More whistleblowers can be expected to come forward with serious public concerns.

The Organization of the Book

The next chapters will lead the reader into the complex world of whistleblowing. Chapter 2 will explore how individuals make the decision to blow the whistle, while Chapter 3 investigates the conditions required for whistleblowers to actually succeed in changing policy. Chapter 4 illustrates how an agency has "improved" as a result of the efforts of a whistleblower, and the focus of Chapter 5 is legal protection. Finally, Chapter 6 expands into the global arena, describing how the United States' support of whistleblowing is having a worldwide impact.

Notes

1. The "wrongdoing" Congress had in mind when it protected whistleblowers' free speech in the 1978 Civil Rights Reform Act was "illegality, abuse of authority, mismanagement, gross waste or substantial and specific danger to public health or safety" (Civil Service Reform Act of 1978, PL 95-454).
   In 1992, the General Accounting Office, in their Whistleblower Protection survey of federal employees (GAO/GGD-92-120FS), used the summary term *misconduct* to define a protected disclosure under law (5 U.S.C. 2302 [b] [8] A). They defined it as "a violation of any law, rule, or regulation; gross mismanagement; gross waste of funds; abuse of authority; or acts of substantial and specific danger to public health and safety."
2. "While it was not an entirely new phenomenon for insiders to expose scandal within their organizations, according to David Bollier, "the [1971] conference helped give the behavior a new name and identity—'whistleblowing'—and publicly legitimized the behavior."
3. *Serpico*, a 1973 film directed by Sidney Lumet, stars Al Pacino, Tony Roberts, and John Randolph; *Silkwood* is a 1984 film directed by Mike Nichols, starring Meryl Streep, Kurt Russell and Cher; *Marie*, a 1986 film directed by Roger Donaldson, stars Sissy Spacek and Keith Szarabajka.
4. James Q. Wilson, in *Bureaucracy* (1989), describes how professionals hired to work in government agencies can bring with them the distinct cultural values of their profession. He calls these "professional norms" and "beliefs" (pp. 86–88). Professional standards, of course, can vary and are not guaranteed to stimulate whistleblowing. CPAs are an example. On January 19, 2002, with the backdrop of the Arthur Andersen and Enron scandals, *San Francisco*

Chronicle reporter Arthur M. Louis argued that CPAs, as a professional group, are *not* likely to be whistleblowers; they are more likely to quit their jobs. "When auditors unearth accounting behavior that they consider fishy," Louis wrote, "and if they can't get their management to make changes, their normal practice is to resign the account without fanfare" (Louis 2002: B-1, B-2).

5. "As millions of Americans were filing their returns on tax day [April 1999], the Houston office of the IRS was in the process of firing the first internal revenue agent to publicly blow the whistle about agency abuses," reported the *New York Times*. Jennifer Long had been served with a letter, a sixty-day warning that was tantamount to a notice that she would be fired. Twenty-three hours later, the letter was withdrawn because the chair of the Senate Finance Committee, Senator William Roth, protested the action to the new tax commissioner, Charles Rossoti. Two years later, the Associated Press reported a similar intervention. In February 2001, IRS officials did not fill out a routine character form for Jennifer Long to be sent to the Texas licensing regulators. Instead, they sent them a letter critical of whistleblower Jennifer Long's work. But Republican senator Charles Grassley, new chair of the Senate Finance Committee, wrote to the IRS commissioner of his concern that their criticism of Long to the Texas licensing regulators looked like a first step toward her termination in retaliation for her testimony as a congressional witness. The critical IRS letter was never sent.

6. In order to attract and enhance their image and with it public support, government agencies have even collaborated with television and movie producers. While there is a history of such cooperation from the FBI and the Pentagon (J. Edgar Hoover was very involved with the TV series *The FBI*, and the Pentagon helped the filmmakers of *Top Gun* and *The Hunt for Red October*), the CIA is now working "regularly with filmmakers, television producers and writers it considers sympathetic," according to Elaine Sciolino in the *New York Times*. The CIA headquarters in Langley, Virginia, are even being used for a CBS-TV series, *The Agency*.

7. In the months just following September 11, surveys found U.S. citizens significantly less cynical. Responding differently to questions about trust, 51 percent "expressed greater confidence in the federal government in 2001 than they had a year earlier" (Putnam 2002). But these survey results also suggested that this new mood of trust expressed itself "primarily through images" and not with a fundamental change in civic practice. For example, "much of the measurable increase in generosity spent itself within a few weeks" after September 11 (Putnam 2002). Therefore, it is not at all clear that an increased feeling of public trust in government (post–September 11) will continue; the old cynicism is likely to be lurking beneath the surface.

8. Using the standard definition of whistleblowing, Sherron Watkins was not technically a whistleblower; when she wrote her memo, she did not intend for her concerns about Enron practices to be exposed to the public and to the press.

2

Deciding to Become a Whistleblower

G overnment surveys show that only a fraction of federal employees
who observe illegal or wasteful activities report and expose them
(U.S. Merit Systems Protection Board 1984: 3). I wonder how many of
these thousands of employees still remember their decision not to act.
Weisband and Franck suggest that "each time we acquiesce, by 'playing
up' rather than speaking up, we raise the threshold of our moral outrage" (Weisband and Franck 1975: 8). How many might wish another
chance to blow the whistle if they had a video with a choice of endings?

Albert Camus imagined a "second chance" in *The Fall*. At the end
of his book, Camus describes how a prominent lawyer has an unexpect-
ed choice to make. A young woman jumps from a bridge and the lawyer
fails to respond to her cries as she drowns. He is haunted by the failure
of not rescuing her; he desperately wants another chance to save her but
he fears that he won't be up to the task. "O young woman, throw yourself into the water again so that I may a second time have the chance of
saving both of us!" And then he realizes what he is asking for. "A second time, eh, what a risky suggestion! Just suppose . . . that we should
be taken literally? We'd have to go through with it. Brr . . . ! The
water's so cold!" (1969: 147).[1]

Similarly, blowing the whistle on wrongdoing is risky business.
Nevertheless, some decide to take the plunge. How do they make their
decision?

When one asks people why they are, or are not, whistleblowers,
their explanations almost always mention consequences. This chapter
explores the thinking that underlies a whistleblower's decision and how
potential whistleblowers might calculate the consequences of their

25

actions. Two cases give us an insider's view of whistleblowing and a rich enough narrative to be able to apply an ethics checklist. Since strong feelings of loyalty to agency, career, profession, or principle might enter into the assessment, we first need to examine the idea of loyalty.

Exploring Loyalty

It is a rare whistleblower case where those involved do not bring up the issues of loyalty and disloyalty. When we feel loyal to a friend or to the agency where we work, it flows from our relationship with them. Loyalty to organization is usually expected and valued. As Sissela Bok points out, "Fidelity to one's agency, to one's superiors, and to colleagues is stressed in countless ways." Therefore, it is no surprise that a whistleblower, whose public revelations often embarrass his or her agency, is usually seen as disloyal because, while "neither referee nor coach," he or she is blowing the whistle "on his [or her] own team" (Bok 1981: 207).

We grow up learning the value of loyalty to our family, playmates, classmates, colleagues—to our group. This brand of loyalty runs deep. It presumes an experience of "bonding" and even as far back as Aristotle's description of loyalty, it presupposed a relationship "rooted in shared histories" (Fletcher 1993: 7).

Our feelings of loyalty have even been the subject of film. Among the numerous examples are *Somebody Up There Likes Me*, *On the Waterfront*, *A Bronx Tale*, *Music Box*, and the made-for-TV film series *The Sopranos*.[2] Some of these movies illustrate moral struggle, while in others loyalty is a given, and the characters only want to avoid being seen as disloyal "tattle-tales" or "squealers."

When we are grown and working, it is usually presumed that we will be loyal to our co-workers and to our organization—a sentiment captured by an old German saying, "Whose bread I eat, his song I sing" (Branch 1979: 217), and a sentiment also captured by a former government employee who said, "Being a Democrat or Republican is just a party affiliation. 'Don't make waves' is a religion" (Isbell 1977: 75).

But we also grow up learning something else—that there is a "right" and "wrong," and in the United States, this message is reinforced for government employees. As described in Chapter 1, in 1980 Congress unanimously provided a Code of Ethics requiring that government personnel "put loyalty to the highest moral principle above loyalty to persons, party, or government department."[3] This edict has been characterized as creating a hierarchy of loyalties. It has also been pointed out that we might not all buy into this hierarchy. Albert Camus's comment is a famous example. He was alleged to have said, "I believe in justice, but I will defend my mother before justice" (Fletcher 1993: 154).

So, here are two opposing pressures: the traditional pressure to be loyal to one's organization, and the government code's requirements to be loyal to the highest moral principle, or as Bok states it, "loyalty to the agency and to colleagues comes to be pitted against loyalty to the public interest" (1981: 207). Nearly a hundred years ago, Josiah Royce tried to use the principle of loyalty itself as a guide for clarifying such contradictory expectations.[4]

As a Harvard professor and a leading proponent of philosophical idealism, Josiah Royce, in *The Philosophy of Loyalty*, tried to inspire people to appreciate loyalty (1908: vii, 120). He saw loyalty as devotion to a cause (p. 16), and as a relative term because ultimately its value comes from the causes to which loyalty is shown. The way we choose between loyalties, he suggested, is to choose the cause that is more compelling (pp. 42, 47).

In *The Philosophy of Loyalty*, Royce expressed hope that individuals would understand the significance of deciding between loyalties and not automatically choose what is traditionally expected (pp. 120, 122). However, he recognized that we are imperfect, "imitative, plastic, and in bitter need of ties" (p. 124).

Loyalty not only defines us but can connect us to the community in different ways. Considering the fitting objects of loyalty, Royce recognized that the "cause" might be your career but it could also be "much larger than your private self" and connect many individuals (pp. 19, 20). Royce offered a principle that, while sounding a little arcane today,[5] might provide guidance when choosing between two causes. "In so far as it lies in your power," he said, "so choose your cause and so serve it, that, by reason of your choice and of your service, there shall be more loyalty in the world rather than less" (p. 21). This represents being loyal to loyalty.

Royce made a very practical contribution by inviting us to view our conflicts between principle and agency affiliation as *conflicts of loyalty*. By framing the decision as one between loyalties to different causes, we are no longer weighing principle against loyalty but are invited to compare causes we are loyal to. And in an interesting way, Royce's recasting of the decision as one between loyalties makes a subtle but significant modern-day contribution when we relate what he says to the usually deteriorated relationship between whistleblower and co-worker.

Whistleblowers are usually ostracized and punished by their former friends and colleagues, and almost certainly by their agencies. In return, many whistleblowers dismiss with disdain, and with a kind of moral smugness, their "less courageous" co-workers who don't come forward. Adopting Royce's idea of loyalty might help change this interplay. Ironically, he would likely demand from the whistleblower, as well as from those who stand by quietly because of loyalty toward agency, an expression of respect. They are all, he says, "children of one spirit." They are all, after all, exercising loyalty.

> The principle of loyalty to loyalty . . . requires you *to respect loyalty in all men, wherever you find it.* If your fellow's cause has, in a given case, assailed your own, and if, in the world as it is, conflict is inevitable, you may then have to war with your fellow's cause, in order to be loyal to your own. But even then, you may never assail whatever is sincere and genuine about his spirit of loyalty. . . . All the loyal are brethren. They are children of one spirit. Loyalty to loyalty involves the active furtherance of this spirit wherever it appears. (pp. 157–158)

And so, if Royce had his way, the whistleblower would be required to respect his or her co-workers' sense of loyalty to agency and to team, loyalty to family, career, and personal interest. At the same time, they, in turn, would need to view the whistleblower not as someone who is disloyal, but as someone loyal to another cause. Presumably, if the exercise of loyalty were respected, it might increase the level of civility, the ability to communicate, and possibly in some cases the ability to find compromise between agency co-workers and whistleblowers.

Sissela Bok, a contemporary philosopher and social critic, is also interested in preserving civility. She argues that the act of whistleblowing can be so damaging to programs, agencies, and to the people involved that the consequences of acting must be very carefully weighed. Bok crafts a framework on consequences that is offered as a kind of checklist for the potential whistleblower.[6]

It is important to note that concerns about consequences, such as those Bok outlines, and concerns about loyalty, such as those expressed by Royce, present different kinds of moral considerations. The demand of loyalty to a principle, for example, can feel emotional and "uncompromisable," while concerns about consequences require calculations about empirical matters.

Weighing the Consequences

In her essay "Blowing the Whistle," Bok (1981) suggests that whistle-blowers ought to be aware of their moral responsibility and carefully weigh the consequences of their decisions. She dissects the act of whistleblowing, slicing it into three elements: dissent, breach of loyalty, and accusation. These elements provide the framework with which to discuss possible harms and benefits and from these elements flow a distinct set of issues and questions to help in the decisionmaking process. For Bok, approaching whistleblowing in this manner forces an individual to examine a range of issues while weighing their moral implications.

Dissent: The subject of the whistleblower's dissent, unlike other dissenters, is narrow and concerns negligence, abuse, and public risk. Because those who dissent on these grounds believe they do so to benefit the public, whistleblowers have an obligation to consider the nature of this promised benefit as they weigh the possible harm that may come to persons, institutions, and the public itself from their speaking out. For Bok, those thinking about blowing the whistle must consider the accuracy of the facts they have gathered: How serious is the impropriety? How imminent is the threat they warn about? How closely linked is the wrongdoing to those accused of doing it?

Loyalty: For Bok, because whistleblowers breach loyalty to their agency and colleagues, whistleblowing is viewed as a last alternative. Still, she argues, whistleblowing ought to be an option when there is no time to go through routine channels, when institutions are so corrupt or coercive that they would automatically silence the whistleblower, or when there are no internal channels available for bringing the problem to light.

Accusation: Publicly accusing people of serious wrongdoing requires that the whistleblower meet a number of ethical obligations, according to Bok. Potential whistleblowers must consider the fairness of their accusations for the persons being accused; they must consider whether the public is entitled to this information; they must consider their responsibility and not choose anonymity, if at all possible. Most important, they must do some soul searching about their own motives,

Figure 2.1   The Whistleblower Checklist

Dissent: when whistleblowers claim their dissent will achieve a public good, they must ask

- √ What is the nature of the promised benefit?
- √ How accurate are the facts?
- √ How serious is the impropriety?
- √ How imminent is the threat?
- √ How closely linked to the wrongdoing are those accused?

Loyalty: when whistleblowers breach loyalty to their organization, they must ask

- √ Is whistleblowing the last and only alternative?
- √ Is there no time to use routine channels?
- √ Are internal channels corrupted?
- √ Are there no internal channels?

Accusation: when whistleblowers are publicly accusing others, they must ask

- √ Are accusations fair?
- √ Does the public have a right to know?
- √ Is the whistleblower *not* anonymous?
- √ Are the motives *not* self-serving?

Derived from Bok 1981.

watching for feelings of bias, revenge, inflated expectations, and desire for personal gain.

There are many whistleblowers who demonstrate in their public statements not only a loyalty to principle but an appreciation of dire consequences if they don't act. Roger Boisjoly, whose whistleblowing in 1986 exposed the causes of the *Challenger* disaster, and Cindy Ossias, whose whistleblowing in 2000 toppled the corrupt California state commissioner of insurance, are two examples. Applying Sissela Bok's checklist to both of these cases allows us to evaluate the basis of their decisions.

Roger Boisjoly and the Space Shuttle *Challenger*

Roger Boisjoly was a Morton Thiokol engineer. He and other engineers were concerned about the seals that connected solid rocket booster joints on NASA's space shuttle orbiter. After the *Challenger* tragedy, Boisjoly became a whistleblower intent on exposing the agency's prelaunch decisionmaking process, which minimized these safety concerns.

The planned date of launch of the space shuttle *Challenger* (Mission 51-1) was January 23, 1986. But the launch was rescheduled and postponed numerous times to accommodate the late launch of another shuttle (Mission 61-1), minor problems with an exterior hatch handle, and the weather. The day of the flight, problems with a fire detector in the liquid hydrogen ground storage tank caused a delay in the fueling and crew wake-up call. By 8:36 A.M., the crew had left their quarters, ridden the astronaut van to the launch pad, and were in their seats, waiting for ice to melt and for a last ice inspection of the exterior of their craft.

"Flight of the Space Shuttle Challenger on Mission 51-1 began at 11:38 A.M. Eastern Standard Time on January 28, 1986. It ended 73 seconds later in an explosive burn of hydrogen and oxygen propellants that destroyed the External Tank and exposed the Orbiter to severe aerodynamic loads that caused complete structural breakup. All seven crew members perished" (Presidential Commission on the Space Shuttle Challenger 1986: 19). Because the launch was televised, the tragedy could be shared and relived again and again.

Newscasts across the country replayed the shocking image of the exploding space shuttle with video of the confused and frightened onlookers and family members sitting in the bleachers near the launch pad, and with video of the frightened faces of children in classrooms that had tuned in to see the historic launch that carried, for the first time, a teacher-turned-astronaut. The nation mourned the loss collectively.

Six days after the failed launch, President Ronald Reagan established a commission, headed by William Rogers, to investigate the *Challenger* accident. The Rogers Commission concluded in their report on June 6, 1986, that the "loss of the Space Shuttle Challenger was caused by a failure in the joint. . . . The specific failure was the destruction of the seals that are intended to prevent hot gases from leaking through the joint during the propellant burn of the rocket motor" (Presidential Commission on the Space Shuttle Challenger 1986: 40). The public would come to learn a lot about the failed seals that were rubber-like "O-rings" the thickness and color of licorice, twelve feet around, lying "between the booster segments much like the rubber ring between a Mason jar and its lid" (Vaughan 1996: 40).

Roger Boisjoly was one of the Morton Thiokol engineers who alerted his superiors to the potential problem of the predicted cold weather compromising the seal of the O-rings. He was especially concerned about a possible disaster because he was haunted by the experience of a colleague at another company who had worked on the doors of a commercial aircraft, the DC-10.

Boisjoly remembered that, after a crash of a DC-10, "when the DC-10 doors imploded, killing more than three hundred people in Europe, this gentleman suffered terribly. His perception was that he had not done enough to stop the certification of the design, knowing, from an engineering standpoint, that it should not have been certified under its present operating conditions" (Mertzman and Madsen 1992: 47). That experience was a marker for Boisjoly that he had better not "let the situation with the space shuttle boosters go unattended" (p. 47).

On July 31, 1985, Boisjoly wrote a letter to Morton Thiokol expressing his concerns and warning of a catastrophe. He had two kinds of fears. One, he says, "was the fear for the loss of life and the project. But another was a personal fear, that of being like my colleague, the design engineer [of the DC-10] who had allowed the certification process to go forward when he felt the design was inadequate. While he [his friend] had fought against it, he felt that . . . [his friend] had not fought hard enough" (p. 47).

For years, the seals had been an ongoing concern, not just for

Boisjoly but for many of the engineers, and since August 1985, the O-ring seals were under study by a Morton Thiokol task force. In September 1985, the task force asked NASA for data on the ambient temperature of each launch. Although the information, according to Boisjoly, was available in the logs of the Kennedy Space Center, the task force was not given the information requested (Boisjoly 2001c).

Because of the engineers' safety concerns about O-ring resiliency and their alarm that the *Challenger* flight would go as scheduled on that unusually cold Florida morning, the day before launch, a three-locations telephone conference was arranged at 5:25 P.M. (Eastern Standard Time) involving Morton Thiokol in Utah, Marshall Space Flight Center at Huntsville, Alabama, and the Kennedy Space Center in Florida (Presidential Commission on the Space Shuttle Challenger 1986: 104–110).

At this initial teleconference, Morton Thiokol expressed concerns about the effect of the low temperature on the O-rings in the joint seal. None of the Morton Thiokol engineers participating at this meeting wanted to fly outside their database, the cutoff point of which was 53 degrees Fahrenheit. Morton Thiokol recommended that the launch be delayed. When a contractor recommends against launching, there is usually no launch.

But this delay did not stand for long. Another teleconference was arranged for 8:15 P.M. to include more personnel and to send relevant Morton Thiokol data to all participants. According to Boisjoly, the engineers had about forty-five minutes to prepare for the flight readiness review. They ran to their respective offices and grabbed what they could. In all, they had fourteen view graphs (Boisjoly 2001c).

At 8:45 P.M., a second teleconference took place. The O-ring problem was discussed until 10:30 P.M. when a recess was called to allow for an off-line discussion between Morton Thiokol management and its engineers.

Off line, Morton Thiokol revisited the data concerning temperature's effects on the O-rings and the history of O-ring erosion. Boisjoly characterized this meeting as one "where the determination was to launch, and it was up to us [the engineers] to prove beyond a shadow of a doubt that it was not safe to do so" (Presidential Commission on the Space Shuttle Challenger 1986: 93). The problem for the engineers was that, at the time of the launch, they did not have all relevant information. According to Boisjoly, Larry Mulloy asked for probability numbers but "he knew we didn't have them" (Boisjoly 2001a). The Morton Thiokol engineers did not have *proof* that the seal would fail. It had not, after all, failed in the five previous launches.

When the teleconference resumed, the Thiokol managers reversed the decision. They now recommended launch. The data, they said, was inconclusive.

How could this happen? How could the engineers' initial concerns have ultimately been ignored? For some, the explanation lies in the engineers' culture. According to James Q. Wilson, the engineers' approach at NASA emphasized "quantitative data and distrusted personal opinions." Lacking the definitive data may have inhibited how forcefully the engineers expressed their launch concerns and how seriously their concerns were taken (Wilson 1989: 62–63).

Also pointing to the "engineers' approach," Diane Vaughn (1996) described NASA as having a technical culture. Technical engineer arguments had to meet "quantitative standards." An acceptable engineering argument had to use all available data and the data had to be consistent with the recommendation. The evidence on the O-rings from prior flights was not completely consistent. Yes, there was evidence of damage to the O-rings in cold temperatures. But tests indicated leakage at 75 degrees Fahrenheit as well. NASA operated in an empirically based and rule-bound environment.

The night before launch, Boisjoly was specifically asked what evidence Thiokol had that O-ring damage in former flights was a result of the cold. Recalling his response, Boisjoly said, "I was asked to quantify my concerns, and I said I couldn't" (Vaughan 1996: 303–304). While Boisjoly's arguments and those of the other engineers sounded serious, they were not considered scientifically sound. They did not have the needed data. They were perceived, according to Wilson, as "hunches" (1989: 62).

NASA's decision to launch was a carefully prescribed formal one, made by decisionmakers on four consecutive levels (Presidential Commission on the Space Shuttle Challenger 1986: 83). It was on the lowest level, IV, where the contractor verifies flight readiness. Level IV was where the discussions and decisions were made about the reliability of the O-ring seals. Although Level IV decisionmakers issued a report, their counterparts on Levels III, II, and I never knew that earlier in the evening, the Morton Thiokol engineers had recommended against launch.

In January 1986, officials at NASA may have felt pressured by public impatience with launches because the prior *Columbia* launch (61-C) set a NASA record for false starts. Boisjoly thought, and still does, that the problem was money—that the space program was "oversold and underfunded" and that safety was "not the priority it should be" (Boisjoly 2001a). Nevertheless, the pressures of time and budget constraints were never found to be the core reason NASA went ahead with the scheduled *Challenger* launch (Vaughan 1996: 46, 47). For the Rogers Commission, and for sociologist Diane Vaughan, who comprehensively studied the launch decision process, the ill-fated decision to launch happened because the engineers' arguments that the O-rings would not properly seal in cold weather did not have the kind of supporting data that would meet NASA's scientific requirements.

Boisjoly was plagued by guilt because of what happened. "Even after trying to stop the launch," he said, "and with the disaster of *Challenger* actually occurring, I still beat myself up for a good six to nine months afterwards, feeling that I had not done enough."

> I could have easily ducked out of the meeting the day before. I could have easily said that it was somebody else's problem; it was not in my direct field of operation at that point. I was a technical specialist and was no longer directly involved with that joint, but at the time I knew more about that joint than anybody else in the program. I just took it upon myself to let them know, with my colleagues, that if they launched under such adverse conditions of temperature, the things in my memo would come to pass. While we could not prove it, we had a high expectation that it would come to pass. Yet afterwards, I still felt the guilt of not having done enough. (Mertzman and Madsen 1992: 47–48)

When the Rogers Commission began to hold closed hearings on February 14, 1986, Boisjoly "handed in the smoking gun memos," including his July 1985 letter about the unsafe O-rings warning Morton Thiokol of a catastrophe of the highest order (Boisjoly 2001c). His testimony also helped expose the NASA process of decisionmaking. He believed that the launch decision was wrong and that those who made it should be held accountable. He freely talked to the commissioners and to the public at large, and in the process became a whistleblower. He was guilt ridden and he wanted to prevent another accident.

Boisjoly believed he was more forthcoming in testimony than the other two engineers who participated in the closed hearings (Boisjoly 2001a). The testimony of all three impacted their work and careers; they were all demoted (Clark 2002).

As a result of testifying, Boisjoly said, "my career ended up in the toilet big-time" (Boisjoly 2001b).

> As far as my career, we were told in no uncertain terms by the CEO of Morton Thiokol that we had done the company more harm by answering those questions to the commission in closed hearings than all of the previous press releases to that time. Everything went downhill from there. They made my life a living hell on a day-to-day basis. Here I was, a competent engineer who had plenty to offer, but I was not allowed to contribute. I was being denigrated day after day, in meetings and telephone conversations, not allowed to do what I do best, which is the design work on that type of structure.
>
> It was so devastating to me. I started to have all the physical symptoms of cardiac arrest and/or heart attack. I left the company, at the advice of the company executive, for an extended sick leave to try and calm down to get things back together. While I was away, I got professional help and was diagnosed as having post-traumatic stress disorder as a result of my interface with Morton Thiokol. I called them in September of 1986, and told them I would never return to work. (Mertzman and Madsen 1992: 48–49)

In blowing the whistle, Boisjoly believed he was being loyal to ethical principles. "You are required by ethics," he said. "If you don't do the right thing, you are not doing what you were hired to do" (Boisjoly 2001c). Asked if he would be a whistleblower again, Boisjoly answered, "I would do it again in a minute. . . . If it cost me my job, if it cost me status, or if it cost me a raise, I would do it exactly the same again. I did nothing wrong" (Mertzman and Madsen 1992: 49).

It did cost him his job. Although, at first, Boisjoly believed that he could never work again as an engineer because he feared that he might go through an experience similar to the one with *Challenger*, by 1989 he felt he would be able to handle engineering responsibilities. But the industry branded him a whistleblower, which he said, in the industrial and government setting, connoted "a snitch, a troublemaker, and a malcontent—all of the negatives that are associated with somebody who does something like I did" (p. 49). He opened up his own professional consulting business, specializing in "ethics matters" such as product liability and trade secret cases, where he was his "own boss," accountable only to himself (Boisjoly 2001c).

Even though he personally suffered, Boisjoly believed that the general benefits of his whistleblowing far outweighed the harm done to himself and his career. But what about the other "tests" that Sissela Bok outlines? What about his responsibility to others, including co-worker and agency? How much integrity did his decision have in terms of her checklist?

Applying Bok's Checklist

Dissent: Boisjoly qualifies as a whistleblower because his dissent was over the safety and risks for future launches. He did not have to carry a burden of proving imminent threat; the disaster had already occurred. He was interested in indicting individuals as well as the system that produced the flawed decision. In fact, a year after the tragedy, Roger Boisjoly filed two suits against Morton Thiokol and NASA, by implication, for supplying the defective parts causing the death of the crew members (Vaughan 1996: 45).[7]

There were a number of reasons why Boisjoly did not initially go outside the organization to warn about the problems with the O-rings long before the *Challenger* disaster. First, like Bok, he believed going outside should always be the last alternative. Second, there was movement within the organization, although slowgoing. "At least they had a team to study the problem," he said, and "this created opportunity and hope." Third, while there had been clear evidence that cold weather was responsible for causing massive amounts of damage in two booster joints in the January 1985 launch, the possibility of another day that cold was "one in a hundred years," he said. And fourth, he calculated that there was little chance of success going outside the agency; the media did not want to bring NASA down (Boisjoly 2001b).

When the engineers' "no launch" recommendation was reversed, on the day before the launch, why didn't Boisjoly go outside the agency to stop the launch then? Again, Boisjoly believed he had no chance of success going outside. "If I couldn't convince *those who knew*, what good would going outside do?" (2001b).

After the failed launch, what harms and benefits did he calculate his actions and testimony would produce? Boisjoly never considered the harm his whistleblowing might cause to institutions and the damage he might do to the reputations of Morton Thiokol and NASA. It never crossed his mind, he said, to take the organization's interest into account. His motive was to correct a wrong (2001b).

Following his testimony, Boisjoly was surprised when he was ostracized by the agency. Managers saw what he did as a harmful breach of loyalty. Did Boisjoly believe it necessary for him to breach loyalty and expose personnel decisions and the internal process for the process to change? Absolutely.

Boisjoly believed the basic problem he revealed, which was at the core of launch safety, would continue to go unrecognized without his revelations. The problem, as he saw it, was safety's low priority. The agency had reversed the burden of proof for safety. He said in testimony that "the determination was to launch, and it was up to us to prove beyond a shadow of the doubt that it was not safe to do so. This is in total reverse to what the position usually is in pre-flight conversation or a Flight Readiness Review. It is usually exactly opposite that" (Vaughan 1996: 338). For Boisjoly, articulating and exposing this fundamental and flawed NASA guiding principle was far more important than considering the possible damage done to agency reputation.

Loyalty: For Boisjoly, was disloyalty and the consequence of harming reputations the only way the sought-after benefits could have been achieved? Yes. Boisjoly was not at all loyal to the reputation and image of his company and the agency he worked for. He accused NASA of being "hell-bent on a launch" and of pressuring his management. Boisjoly believed that change within the agency would not come quietly and as a natural result of the *Challenger* calamity, without whistleblowing. NASA needed public exposure and embarrassment before substantially changing its fundamental and underlying values. NASA's immediate response to *Challenger* seemed to reinforce Boisjoly's position.

After the shuttle destruction, NASA acted somewhat suspiciously. They tried to control information related to the shuttle program. NASA impounded documents and instructed its employees, former employees, and officials in private companies involved in the program not to talk to reporters, even on an off-the-record basis. They explained their actions as trying to minimize speculation on the cause of the accident (Jones 1986: 30).

On Thursday, February 6, during the first day of the commission's televised hearings, NASA officials reported on their in-house investigation. They did not focus on the O-rings as a probable cause of the accident and in one testimony the O-rings were downplayed and data on the erosion of secondary seals was misrepresented (Vaughan 1996: 9). Whether it was due to oversight or cover-up, NASA's approach at this time was misleading the commission.

By the end of the weekend, however, the focus and tenor of the commission's investigation had been changed by insider information. Information leaked to the press contradicted NASA's position and gave NASA the appearance of possibly being involved in some sort of cover-up. Based on anonymous NASA sources and inconsistent with NASA's public testimony, Saturday's NBC-TV nightly news reported that NASA's in-house investigation was focused on a possible leak in a joint of the right booster rocket.

The next day, February 9, the Sunday *New York Times* published a front-page story based on leaked NASA documents from Richard Cook at NASA (Boisjoly 2001a) that announced with screaming headlines, "NASA Had Warning of a Disaster Risk Posed by Booster." The article suggested that O-ring failure was the cause of the tragedy, that there were twelve similar instances during previous flights where there had been erosion of the primary O-ring at the seam, and that engineers had warned of this problem the year before. It was information made public by unofficial insider sources that shifted the commission's inquiry.

Now, the commission proceeded with their investigation in closed session and it was only at this point that the commission learned that Morton Thiokol had initially recommended against the launch. Upon learning this, they scheduled interviews with Roger Boisjoly and the other participants in the eve-of-launch teleconference. The way NASA released information six weeks later on how the crew died also reinforced the appearance of a NASA cover-up (Vaughan 1996: 43).

Accusation: For Boisjoly, public exposure was the only effective route to take to prevent such an accident from happening again. He believed NASA's "mindset" was not changed, and would not be changed by the *Challenger* accident alone (Boisjoly 2001c). Boisjoly accused without anonymity. Without question, the public had a right to hear him. The public mourned the loss of the *Challenger* and her crew; they deserved to know why it happened.

But wasn't there a confluence between his service to the public and his own needs? Besides wanting to prevent another accident, Boisjoly needed to allay his guilt and publicly explain how he tried to stop the launch and why he failed. By serving his own needs as well as the public's, his motives may not have quite reached Bok's high exclusively public-serving standards. Nevertheless, if his actions helped to prevent a similar disaster, then as Bok herself admits, sometimes exposés are warranted no matter the motive (Bok 1981: 214).

Another case that helps give us an insider's view of the whistleblower decision is that of Cindy Ossias, an attorney and senior staff counsel in the Legal Division of the California State Department of Insurance. She came forward with information about secret arrangements the California commissioner of insurance had made with six insurance companies related to claims from the 1994 Northridge earthquake. The arrangements deprived many of the earthquake victims of compensation, services, and redress that should have been available to them. Her insider information ultimately caused the commissioner, a rising star in the California Republican Party, to resign, and the department's corruption to stop.

Cindy Ossias and the Northridge Earthquake

On January 17, 1994, five seconds before the clock struck 4:31 A.M. (Pacific Standard Time), an earthquake violently shook the ground northwest of Los Angeles for fifteen seconds. Its epicenter was one mile south-southwest of Northridge and so it soon became known as "the Northridge quake." Its magnitude was 6.7.

Luckily, the earthquake hit during the early morning hours and on the holiday of Martin Luther King Day, so there were fewer fatalities and most manufacturing and service industries were closed. Still, it was one of the costliest natural disasters in U.S. history. It affected the densely populated San Fernando Valley: seventy-two people died; 1,500 were seriously injured; and major freeways were damaged and parts collapsed, forcing the closure of portions of eleven major roads to downtown Los Angeles.

Because the center of the earthquake was mostly residential, the bulk of the structural damage was to residential dwellings; in fact, fully 92 percent of this earthquake's damage was to apartment buildings.

California had had its share of recent disasters. In 1989, the Loma Prieta earthquake radiated destruction and death from the Santa Cruz epicenter to the San Francisco Bay area. In 1991, the Oakland–Berkeley Hills fire left some people dead and thousands homeless, as did the Los Angeles fires of 1993. Huge numbers of settlements with insurance companies followed each disaster. A legacy of insurance company improprieties after these events caused the California Department of Insurance (DOI) to promise vigilance, assistance, and redress of illegal claim practices, to the insured. Government, they promised, would be on the side of the citizen.

In 1994, the victims of the Northridge earthquake hoped for fairness from their insurers and failing that, they expected help from the DOI if they experienced problems. More than 600,000 claims were filed following the quake, which eventually resulted in $15 billion in insured losses (Howard 2000).

In November 1994, Republican candidate Chuck Quackenbush was elected commissioner of insurance. Almost immediately, Quackenbush rewrote the department's mission statement, redefining the insurance companies as "customers" (Ossias 2001a) and the level of department enforcement changed.

Instead of vigorous enforcement, Quackenbush created "unusual" settlement practices with the insurers. In exchange for reducing penalties, insurers were required to provide money for special funds for consumer aid and earthquake damage research. But none of the funds were actually spent in this way. Instead, they paid for projects designed to benefit Quackenbush politically. In 1997 and 1998, the DOI collected $2.5 million in outreach payments and $688,312 in fines for these funds.

The commissioner and the agency alone had discretion over how to spend this money, eliminating from the process the legislature and the governor who usually exercise fiscal oversight (California State Assembly Committee on Insurance 2000: 3). In 1998, thanks, in part, to the benefits of the free TV commercials that the special funds paid for, Quackenbush was reelected commissioner.

By February 1999, the method of subverting funds from settlements with insurers became even more elaborate. A public-relations firm (Stoorza Communications) devised a plan for Quackenbush to establish two foundations into which he would divert funds from insurance companies. The foundations would give the DOI more control over the funds and enable them to use the money for "media campaigns and community-based efforts designed to strengthen Mr. Quackenbush's standing" (p. 3).

Hundreds of thousands of dollars of the foundation money went to social service groups and minority community and other projects. For example, money was distributed to the Sacramento Urban League, to Quackenbush's chief political adviser as a consulting fee, and to a football camp attended by Quackenbush's sons. Millions were spent for television public service spots featuring Quackenbush, including one in which he posed as an NBA referee with Laker star Shaquille O'Neal (Ellis and Tempest 2000).[8]

Thus, at the same time that Quackenbush drastically reduced the penalties insurers paid, he was ensuring that whatever money was collected benefited himself. So blatant were these arrangements that a DOI official testified that "he was told to reach settlements with title insurance companies because Insurance Commissioner Chuck Quackenbush 'needs $4 million for a media buy'" (Smith and Hoge 2000).

Within weeks of the foundations' creation, Commissioner Quackenbush used strong-arm tactics to extract donations to his foundations from Northridge insurers. The following is a shocking and detailed description of his meeting with them from the June 2000 report of the California State Assembly Committee on Insurance:

> In early March 1999, six carriers received administrative subpoenas to appear at DOI. The DOI had been conducting market conduct examinations (MCEs) on four of the insurers—State Farm, Allstate, 21st Century and Farmer's Home Group—to determine whether, and to what extent, they had engaged in unlawful claims practices following the earthquake. Two of the insurers, Fireman's Fund and Farmer's, had not been the subject of MCEs.
>
> Despite their different circumstances, DOI officials treated all six insurers the same at the March 1999 settlement sessions. They threatened the insurers with extremely negative publicity and billions of dollars in fines. They confronted the insurers with fake news stories. They lined the room with empty cardboard boxes to make it appear DOI processed massive documentation and was ready to take the cases to court. (California State Assembly Committee on Insurance 2000: 4)

The donations the DOI demanded fell far short of what the Northridge insurers should have been asked to pay. The DOI lawyers, who had recommended a fine of $119 million for State Farm alone, had been frozen out of these settlement negotiations; Cindy Ossias, one of the agency attorneys, had even been asked by the DOI deputy commissioner to shred agency documents that recommended these huge fines (Salladay 2000).

In truth, the payments these insurers avoided having to make for improper action in Northridge might have totaled as much as $3.7 billion in fines (Gledhill 2000). Instead, Quackenbush reached a settlement with all six Northridge companies to pay a measly $12.5 million, aborting market conduct examinations on four of the insurers and agreeing not to conduct them on the other two.

Of the money the DOI collected, only $100,000 represented a fine. Indeed, the rest of the money collected from insurers went into the Quackenbush foundations called "California Insurance Education

Project" (CIEP), which received $1 million from Farmer's, and the "California Research and Assistance Fund" (CRAF), which received over $11 million.

Not only did Quackenbush's associates benefit from the money; he benefited by being featured on television spots and from political polling paid for by these funds. Essentially, money from these funds enabled him to campaign while in office with his personal war chest.

While millions of dollars were drawn from these Northridge insurers, not a penny of restitution money reached the policyholders who were victims of the quake and now were victims of the DOI. State Assembly Insurance Committee chair Jack Scott (D-Altadena), shocked that earthquake victims never benefited from the money collected, later commented, "Where is the Northridge earthquake in this? . . . as far as I know, not one victim has benefited from this fund" (Ellis and Tempest 2000).

Only an insider would know that the money insurers were asked to pay was a fraction of what they should have been paying in penalties. Cindy Ossias, a DOI attorney, was familiar with the "market conduct investigations" of alleged wrongdoing by insurance companies handling claims from the 1994 Northridge earthquake. DOI auditors had found repeated violations where insurers didn't count rooms that were damaged and understated property value. They found evidence of underpayment, misinformation, and missed deadlines (Salladay 2000).

Ossias reported other violations seen firsthand by examiners and DOI lawyers:

> inadequate and even cursory inspection of homes for damage; ridiculously low settlement offers insufficient to pay for needed repairs; unreasonable delays during which policyholders were forced to wrangle for benefits they were entitled to; long periods in which policyholders were out of their homes while repairs were being performed; delayed discovery of the full extent of damage; and unrepaired damage exacerbated by aftershocks, resulting in policyholders living in unsafe structures and their supplemental claims being denied because of a purportedly expired statute of limitations. (Ossias 2000)

Ossias said, "I was appalled. . . . I felt these exams showed violations that were egregious, that warranted hefty fines and restitution to victims. . . . I certainly did not expect the small numbers that were in the final documents and the fact that the money was going to Foundations" (Smith and Hoge 2000). She estimated that the penalties for alleged violations in Northridge by the six insurance companies

should have brought in billions, not the $12.5 million that insurers paid
(Chronicle Sacramento Bureau 2000; Howard 2000).

Ossias knew about levels of enforcement; she knew that fines were
not being assessed; it was the role of the legal department, where she
worked, to routinely review market conduct investigations. The department was no longer looking after the consumer.

So Cindy Ossias leaked copies of the department's Northridge market conduct examinations to a staff member of the State Assembly
Insurance Committee. The records would establish that each of the settlements was in violation of department standards. Remarks from a state
legislative aide confirmed that had Ossias not turned over the reports,
the committee would not have had the firm case against Quackenbush.
"If she had never turned this over, it never would have happened," s/he
said (Anonymous 2001). Newspaper accounts corroborated this. "Those
documents marked the beginning of disclosures about Quackenbush's
settlements with insurance companies and the probe into the formation
of the foundations and their spending" (Smith and Hoge 2000).

Meanwhile, Chuck Quackenbush asked the California Highway
Patrol (CHP), the agency responsible for protecting state office buildings and property (including documents) to investigate who was leaking
material from the office. On June 21, 2000, Cindy Ossias was formally
questioned by two officials from the CHP.

> Finally, the key questions came. "When was the last time you saw the
> documents in question?"
>> "In January or February of this year," I told them.
>> "What was the purpose of your looking at them?"
>> "I wanted to photocopy them." There was a short pause.
>> "Why did you want to photocopy them?"
>> "I wanted to give them to the Legislature," I answered.
>> Their jaws dropped.
>> The captain, who until this point had not asked many questions,
> inquired, "Did you give them to the Legislature?"
>> And I said, "yes."
>> They looked at each other, looked back at me, and one said,
> "We'd like to take a break now." (Ossias 2000)

Cindy Ossias was no longer an anonymous whistleblower.
Commissioner Quackenbush charged her with acting illegally when she
turned over material that, by state law, was supposed to be kept private.
He put her on paid administrative leave and asked the California

Highway Patrol to further investigate whether she had violated attorney-client privilege, which requires of lawyers that they not divulge confidential information. Although the State Assembly Insurance Committee granted Ossias immunity from criminal prosecution in exchange for testimony, which meant she was no longer vulnerable to criminal charges, she still risked losing her license to practice law.

Ossias had understood the possible consequences when she decided to blow the whistle. "At that point, I guess I was willing to take a risk . . . the risk of violating the law, the risk of losing my bar license, the risk of losing my job," she said (Smith and Hoge 2000).

At the end of November, the State Bar of California exonerated her of "any violation of lawyer ethics when she leaked documents that contributed to the downfall of former Insurance Commissioner Chuck Quackenbush." The state bar found that her actions were protected by California's whistleblower act and more important, that she "advanced . . . public policy considerations bearing on the responsibilities of the office of insurance commissioner" (*Los Angeles Times* 2000: A-13).[9]

There were echoes of Josiah Royce when Cindy Ossias struggled with the experience of competing loyalties. "My loyalties were at war last year," she said, "loyalty to my boss, loyalty to the agency, loyalty to the public and loyalty to the rules of professional conduct" (Ellis 2001). She chose the cause that was most compelling.

Applying Bok's Checklist

Dissent: Ossias said she felt "morally compelled to act" because the object of her dissent was abuse of public office (Howard 2000). "Duty and conscience compelled me to act" (Ossias 2000). The good she sought was enormous. Not only was her aim to stop corruption in a department that had been, and was supposed to be, a consumer protection agency. She also wanted to educate the public about their elected officials (Ossias 2001a).

She considered the improprieties serious enough to risk her own career as well as to threaten the careers of those who perpetrated the wrongdoing. Her facts were not only accurate, but the public case depended on them and it was up to her to bring them forward. The wrongdoing was not only closely linked to those accused; it was Ossias's evidence that would give muscle to the investigation that would substantiate the link. More important even than the fact that people did not get the compensation they were due was the fact that the public trust had been violated. Ossias believed she helped restore it.

Loyalty: Unlike almost all other whistleblowers, Cindy Ossias did not feel that she breached loyalty when she blew the whistle. In fact, she insists that she was loyal to her agency and its mission and that she had the consumers' interest at heart when she acted. Ossias had been the department's project counsel, assigned to help survivors of the 1991 Oakland-Berkeley firestorm, the 1993 Los Angeles fires, and the Northridge earthquake of 1994. She felt she was not alone in her dedication. "I work with dedicated public servants," she wrote. "There are lawyers, administrative law judges, investigators, examiners, analysts, support staff in every state agency who want to do the right thing for the citizens for whom they work" (Ossias 2000).

Ossias was a lucky exception when it comes to whistleblowing. She was not isolated, ostracized, and resented by her co-workers. In fact, just the opposite occurred: her feelings about the agency and its corruption were clearly shared by others at DOI.

The day after she was interviewed by the CHP officers who exposed her as the whistleblower, she returned to her San Francisco office where some of her colleagues took her to lunch. When her supervisor informed her that she was to go on administrative leave, asking her to "vacate the premises immediately," by the time she had finished gathering up all her personal items, an entourage of her colleagues, she said, formed to support her on the way to her car. There were hugs and kisses and one colleague told Ossias that she was "her hero" (Ossias 2000). At her old office,

> on the day Ossias testified at legislative hearings, some 20 of her colleagues crowded into a meeting room. . . . Her testimony before two legislative committees was broadcast over an intercom system from Sacramento.
>   No one left the room for the entire time she testified. . . . There were times when a hush would fall all over the room as we waited for her next word. We cheered and high-fived [one of her colleagues reported] when she named names. We were incredibly pleased she was naming people we all knew to be responsible. . . .
>   It was like listening to a sporting event, intense listening followed by occasional eruptions of cheering. (Rutland 2000)

Ossias, referring to her co-workers who were also filled with outrage over the corruption, said, "It was as much for them as for the people of California that I'd leaked the reports" (Ossias 2000). She seemed to have no choice but to go outside her agency. Six years had passed. "There was no way anybody would ever know what these companies had done," she said (Howard 2000).

Who might she have appealed to for consumer restitution or justice when the head of the agency was the wrongdoer? "The man at the top was behind all of this," she said. "There was no point in going up the chain" (Ossias 2001a).

Accusation: At first, Ossias came forward anonymously. But as we saw in her testimony, she was fully prepared to expose her identity during the CHP interrogation. Luckily, she was able to negotiate immunity in exchange for testimony with the State Assembly Committee, thus protecting herself from criminal charges.

According to those who worked with her closely, her motive was public service and what drove her was that she was a "public servant" and believed in consumer rights. Although she was asked about having an anti-Republican bias (which she vigorously denied) when she was questioned at the State Assembly Insurance Committee hearings (Smith and Hoge 2000), such motivation seems unlikely since the bipartisan State Assembly Insurance Committee was unanimous in its conclusions and condemnation of Quackenbush.

Her motives were clear, consistent over time, and well known. But her case, which seems to have satisfied so many of Sissela Bok's ethical concerns, may not be typical, according to Bok. "The ideal case of whistleblowing—where the cause is a just one, where all the less dramatic alternatives have been exhausted, where responsibility is openly accepted, and where the whistleblower is above reproach—is rare" (1981: 214).

Using a Checklist

How useful is an ethics checklist?[10] For observers of whistleblowing, it is a very useful device. It is certainly a helpful evaluative tool after the fact. Evidence also suggests that the thousands of employees who say they have observed agency wrongdoing have done their own calculations before deciding to do nothing; their reasons show that they have seriously weighed the risks (U.S. Merit Systems Protection Board 1984: 3; Sturdivant 1989).

But what of those who decide to blow the whistle? In general, once their decision is made, what is striking in what they say and write is the absence of an element of calculation from their explanations and their stories. Instead of talking about carefully weighing the pros and cons, they are apt to be more like Cindy Ossias who said she felt "morally compelled to act," and Roger Boisjoly who felt "required by ethics" and felt he had no choice.

For whistleblowers, their felt loyalty to principle, their commitment to preventing harm, so outweighed for them all other factors that there was no "deciding." The decision was made. It is what C. Fred Alford calls a "choiceless choice" (2001: 40),[11] and it is captured by Tom Delaney who, as a whistleblower, exposed the failure of the Department of Energy to properly clean an abandoned research site. He said, "I just couldn't stop imagining what would happen if children climbed over the fence and played in the radioactive dust" (p. 66).

These two cases of Roger Boisjoly and Cindy Ossias are vastly different in circumstance, issue, agency, and context. Yet there seems to be an element of inevitability in their stories. Although each might have thought about consequences, the factors that trumped all others did not come from a standardized measure or the experience of calculation. Their decisions were based on a more private, principled consideration.

Decisionmaking in the whistleblowing arena seems to involve a most interesting individualized mix of rational and emotional factors. To believe that whistleblowers make their decisions to expose wrongdoing on an entirely rational basis misrepresents the important ingredient of emotion that all may share. Whether it is a sense of justice or injustice, anger or fear, emotions and values have an impact on, and may override, consequentialist calculations. When Roger Boisjoly was shown Bok's whistleblower checklist, he said he didn't think it would have helped; he *had to do* what he did (Boisjoly 2001b). When Cindy Ossias was shown the checklist, her first response was "this is very rational," and while she admitted that she had asked herself many of the checklist's questions, she nevertheless concluded by saying, "I went largely on my gut. . . . I wish I could say I was more rational" (Ossias 2001c).

Bystander Apathy

These two cases are unique in many ways but they are also like so many other whistleblower cases in an important respect. The whistleblower has been vindicated and the wrongdoing seems, in retrospect, to represent a serious public risk or abuse. It forces us to ask why, if the harm is so clear, there is only one or just a very few whistleblowers who come forward. Those who silently stand by might be demonstrating what has been called "bystander apathy."[12]

The term *bystander apathy* was used and popularized in the mid-1960s because of the murder of Kitty Genovese. In 1964, in Queens, New York, Kitty Genovese was murdered outside her apartment house. It took half an hour to kill her, during which time the killer left and then came back to finish the job. Her screaming was heard by thirty-eight neighbors who watched from windows but did not help her and did not call the police. This event shocked New York and stimulated hundreds of research studies. How can a large number of people witness a wrongdoing and none of them do anything?

Two factors help explain how good people can witness wrongdoing and be bystanders. First, many emergencies are ambiguous and need to be interpreted. This calls into play the second factor. If *others appear unconcerned*, it will likely make you hesitate about reacting—you don't want to embarrass yourself or appear foolish and wrong. In crowds, the larger the crowd, the less likely that anyone will break rank and act (Latané and Darley 1970).

The parallels with whistleblowing are striking. The above two elements are present. There is often *ambiguity* about how to define the situation and there is a similar kind of pressure *not to break rank.* Judge John T. Noonan's 700-page book *Bribes* (1984) illustrates ambiguities about bribery, one kind of wrongdoing. He looks at the bribe in different cultures and different times and suggests that a society often has at least four definitions of a bribe—"that of the more advanced moralist; that of the law as written; that of the law as in any degree enforced; that of common practice." Whether it is a bribe or a gift may not always be clear.

Add to the ambiguity of the situation the fact that others may not appear to see it as a problem, and you have the two (bystander apathy) factors coming together, stopping many people from whistleblowing. This dynamic suggests an intriguing explanation for why many more people do not come forward to blow the whistle.

But even when there is what seems to be clear and unambiguous wrongdoing, most people do not expose it because of what they believe is likely to happen, or not happen, as a result. The effect whistleblowing will have on your job, career, and future is one of the most widely recognized reasons why people do not come forward (U.S. Merit Systems Protection Board 1993: 13; 1984: 3). And it is understandable. Personal interest, self-protection, the quest for promotion, personal favor, opportunity, recognition, and even wealth explain what some bureaucrats seek most of the time, and most bureaucrats seek some of the time. These concerns are well-used standards for action and as Stephen Bailey, in his essay "Ethics in the Public Service," suggests, "there is no way of avoiding the introduction of personal and private interest into the calculus of public decisions" (1988: 464).

Nevertheless, we have come to expect that for public officials, personal gain is not usually their only standard. Even though personal gain is part of the bureaucratic decisionmaking mix, we still expect from the public servant that he or she will use more than just the standards of narrow self-interest when making a public decision, including a decision about whistleblowing. Bailey, describing the bureaucrats, puts it this way, "Man's feet may wallow in the bog of self-interest, but his eyes and ears are strangely attuned to calls from the mountaintop" (p. 465).

Deciding to blow the whistle on wrongdoing is a complex and risky business. But some whistleblowers actually succeed in effecting the change that they risked everything for. The next chapter will systematically explore the environmental factors that make it possible for whistleblowers to succeed in doing this against great odds.

Notes

1. Camus actually ends his short book *The Fall* (1969) by giving up that second chance, saying, "But let's not worry! It's too late now. It will always be too late. Fortunately!" (p. 147).

2. *Somebody Up There Likes Me*, a 1956 film directed by Robert Wise and starring Paul Newman and Pier Angeli; *On the Waterfront*, a 1954 film directed by Elia Kazan and starring Marlon Brando and Eva Marie Saint; *A Bronx Tale*, directed by Robert de Niro, starring Robert de Niro, Chazz Palmiteri, and Joe Pesci; *Music Box*, a 1989 film directed by Costa-Gravas, starring Jessica Lange and Armin Mueller-Stahl; the television series *The Sopranos*, begun in 1999, has had a variety of directors including David Chase, Daniel Attias, Nick Gomez, John Patterson, Lorraine Senna, and Andy Wolk. The starring roles in *The Sopranos* are played by James Gandolfini, Edie Falco, Nancy Marchand, and Dominic Chianese.

3. PL 96-303, unanimously passed by Congress, June 27, 1980.

4. Josiah Royce was a leading proponent of philosophical idealism, a

school of thought that dominated U.S. philosophy until World War I. He was born in Grass Valley, California, on November 20, 1855. He studied engineering at the University of California, and philosophy in Leipzig and Gottingen, Germany, and at Johns Hopkins University, where he received his doctorate in 1878. Royce taught English at the University of California, and in 1885 he became a member of the philosophy department at Harvard University. He published extensively and his effect as teacher and writer has been described as "profound" (*Encyclopedia Britannica*, vol. 19, 1953: 600–601). In fact, a former student at a memorial service for him commemorated Royce's teaching as providing "a clear unclouded landscape of spiritual reality where we sat like gods together but not careless of mankind" (Mead 1917: 170). In a very "American" way, Royce combined idealism, system building, and an appeal to experience. Among Josiah Royce's published works are *The Religious Aspect of Philosophy* (1885), *The Spirit of Modern Philosophy* (1892), *The Conception of God* (1895), *Studies of Good and Evil* (1898), *The World and the Individual* (1900–1901), and *The Philosophy of Loyalty* (1908).

5. As evidence of how "out of fashion" this discussion of loyalty is, we might reflect on C. Fred Alford's recent frustrating search for current books on loyalty, which he describes on page 8 of his book *Whistleblowers' Broken Lives and Organizational Power* (2001). When he visited the web site amazon.com, he found a 250-book list on "loyalty"; over 200 were on consumer and employee loyalty with the most frequent category being "brand loyalty"; twenty of the books were on the loyalty oath, and a few were on Hitler's SS. Only "a couple," he reports, were related to "loyalty as a complex moral virtue."

6. Sissela Bok is not the only author interested in whistleblowing consequences. Marcia P. Miceli and Janet P. Near, in *Blowing the Whistle* (1992), for example, also focus on potential costs and benefits. However, theirs is a more global look with broad calculations that include potential costs and benefits to the employing organization and to the public at large.

7. The Department of Justice would not support the suits, and they were summarily dismissed.

8. The following is a published list of the organizations receiving a total of $5.6 million from Chuck Quackenbush's California Research and Development Foundation. It appeared in Virginia Ellis and Rone Tempest, "Funds Went to Host of Non-Quake Purposes; Insurance: Records Show That Research Foundation Set Up by Quackenbush Gave Hundreds of Thousands to Athletic Programs and Social Service Groups. The Commissioner Defends the Expenditures," *Los Angeles Times*, April 25, 2000, p. A-1: TV spots featuring Quackenbush: $3 million; "Quake Ready" program including children's web site and TV spots featuring Shaquille O'Neal and Quackenbush: $1 million; Sacramento Urban League: $500,000; PACE minority outreach program: $400,000; Skillz Athletics Foundation (football camp): $263,000; 100 Black Men organization: $200,000; Freedom Fund for community development: $100,000; Athletes and Entertainers for Kids: $70,000; 911 4 Kids: $45,000; Oakland Mentoring Center: $40,000; Meadowview Community Assn., Sacramento: $25,000; Community Connections: $18,000; National Latino Peace Officers Assn.: $12,000; Black Film Makers Assn.: $10,000; 2nd District

Education and Policy Foundation (L.A.): $10,000; and Northern California Reinvestment Consortium: $10,000.

9. One of the public policy consequences that was not foreseen was that Ossias's case became a benchmark for crafting extended whistleblower protection for state and private-sector employees in California. Spearheaded by State Senator Jackie Speier, amendments to the California Whistleblower Protection Act (SB 413) strengthened protections by redefining burdens of proof and requiring that notice about whistleblower protection be sent to all state agency employees by e-mail annually. Cindy Ossias testified at the bill's legislative hearings. In addition, Assemblymember Darrell Steinberg took the lead in the California Legislature to carve out guidelines crafting a whistleblower protection law for government attorneys (AB 3634). His efforts were temporarily deferred so that the California State Bar could amend their Rules of Professional Conduct, changes that would require approval from the California Supreme Court. These changes were forthcoming on January 26, 2002, when the California State Bar Board of Governors "approved amendments to the state's Rules of Professional Conduct to authorize lawyers to report serious misconduct by their bosses without breaking attorney-client confidentiality." Mike McKee outlined the changes in his front-page article "Bar Has Guide for Whistlers," in *The Recorder,* January 29, 2002. The amendments to Rule 3-600 would allow government lawyers to go to law enforcement officers or regulatory authorities for serious wrongdoing and to report less serious wrongdoing first to the next-higher authority within their organization, and to outside authorities as a last resort.

As to the fate of former insurance commissioner Chuck Quackenbush, he resigned from his position rather than testify under oath to a state legislature that was considering his impeachment. He and his family moved to Oahu, Hawaii.

10. The widely distributed publication *The Whistleblower's Survival Guide: Courage Without Martyrdom*, produced by the Government Accountability Project (1997), offers a preparedness checklist concerned with legal and practical matters. It also asks the reader whether their issue is substantial enough for the risks, whether the allegations are reasonable and provable, and whether their action will actually help resolve the wrongdoing. It is a guide that prepares the whistleblower for the difficult road ahead.

11. C. Fred Alford would disagree that it is an ethical principle that creates the whistleblower's "choiceless choice." He turns ethical categories into psychological explanations when he argues that, although the whistleblower articulates a commitment to principle, he or she is really blowing the whistle because of a commitment to the principled person he or she is. It is the whistleblower's self-image as an ethical person, Alford believes, that compels him or her to act. He calls it "narcissism moralized" because the content of the ego ideal becomes moral.

12. Marcia P. Miceli and Janet P. Near (1992: 58–59) also explore the parallels of whistleblowing and bystander apathy. They suggest that the thought process that may lead a person to blow the whistle is similar to what happens in bystander intervention.

3

The Whistleblower as Policy Entrepreneur

E very day, whistleblowers expose wrongdoing to journalists and hot-lines hoping to effect a change of behavior in their organizations. Perhaps the Food and Drug Administration has bowed to pressure from the pharmaceutical industry, or the Department of Defense is not audit-ing military contracts carefully enough, or the General Services Administration is allowing government leasing of unsafe buildings. Whistleblowers risk their reputations and careers to expose these prac-tices. Since a whistleblower's aim is to change agency policy or proce-dures, whistleblowers can be thought of as "policy entrepreneurs." According to John W. Kingdon, the defining characteristic of policy entrepreneurs "is their willingness to invest their resources—time, ener-gy, reputation, and sometimes money—in the hope of a future return" (1995: 122). For the whistleblower, the wished-for return comes in the form of changed agency practices.

The description of whistleblowing offered in Chapter 1 provides a definition that enables us to distinguish acts of whistleblowing from other kinds of organizational dissent. The whistleblower is one who succeeds in exposing significant wrongdoing about their agency to the public. Their hope is to change the organization policy. How might we measure their impact on policy?

Policy impact refers to those events occurring after and as a conse-quence of whistleblowing that affect the whistleblower's issue. There are three dimensions of policy impact: (1) the policy agenda, (2) bureaucratic procedures, and (3) substantive public policy.

There are, therefore, three key questions to ask:

53

1. Was there more or less attention paid to the problem? Were new policy alternatives seriously considered by significant political actors? For example, did the whistleblowing mobilize organized interests? Did it affect public opinion? Did it lead to a demand for policy change?
2. What impact did whistleblowing have on conditions in the agency itself? Were there changes in organizational resources? Were there changes in personnel and procedures? Were there changes in the way rules and regulations were implemented?
3. How was substantive public policy affected, as indicated, for example, by public pronouncements or by legislative efforts to formulate or adopt new policies or to clarify existing policy?

All these questions provide a framework to judge whether an act of whistleblowing has had an impact on policy.

Working with whistleblower cases with an eye toward measuring policy impact can be methodologically difficult. Case studies are rooted in different fields, which makes them difficult to compare systematically (Grumm and Wasby 1980: 850–851; Sabatier 1987). Second, variables may not be clear and data may be unavailable or unreliable. Often, so much is happening at the same time whistleblowers are acting that it may be hard to know how much credit to give them. In some cases, whistleblowers may be unduly modest in taking credit for their accomplishments, while in others they may claim far too much. Still, if we can analyze a few whistleblower cases in depth, we can begin to unravel what makes the whistleblower successful. My hypothesis is that a whistleblower's success in influencing policy is not only determined by his or her own characteristics and by the characteristics of the whistleblower issue, but also by the environment.

The characteristics of the whistleblowers may cause them to succeed or fail in affecting policy. Their status in the organization, credibility, and political skills may contribute to their success. In addition, the kinds of issues whistleblowers champion (e.g., their saliency, specificity, and the feasibility of correcting the behavior being criticized) can also contribute to whistleblower success or failure. But just as important as personal and issue characteristics is a factor the whistleblower has little or no control over—the environment. And yet, the environment may be the most important factor of all in effecting organization and policy change.

"Environment" includes the activity of interest groups or advocacy coalitions, public opinion and media attention, and the response of legislators to the accusations of "wrongdoing." These environmental variables are interactive and must be treated as an important context for understanding the whistleblower's success. Successful policy entrepreneurs, with persistence and skill, might be able to move their issues up on the agenda, but Kingdon warns that a single individual's efforts are never solely responsible for his or her success (1995: 180). Thus, it is only when the environment creates a window of opportunity that the whistleblower affects policy. In fact, the hypothesis of this chapter is that whistleblowing is most likely to have a policy impact when several key conditions are met: when media coverage is supportive, sympathetic interest groups work actively to bring about investigations or corrective actions, and legislators are receptive to the charges and are willing to act.

I have selected two well-known cases in the federal government to demonstrate the importance of the whistleblower's environment for success. The cases are atypical. They took place in the 1980s within an unusual historical context. A Republican president, Ronald Reagan, was trying to implement a conservative agenda that included extensive deregulation. Career bureaucrats in the federal agencies, being more liberal than the president, were likely to disagree with such policy goals. A Democratic House of Representatives was also likely to resist the president's efforts. These conditions increased the likelihood of dissent within the bureaucracy as well as the chances that Congress would support the dissenters with well-publicized inquiries and hearings. Nevertheless, however unusual this time period was, the following two cases from this time are useful because they allow us to describe the conditions associated with policy impact and to identify some of the mechanisms of bureaucratic accountability that enhance opportunities for effecting policy change.

The first case involves Hugh Kaufman, who blew the whistle on the Environmental Protection Agency over abuses in hazardous-waste programs; the second focuses on Hal Freeman, San Francisco regional manager, Office for Civil Rights in the Department of Health and Human Services, who blew the whistle over its failure to protect against discrimination individuals who were thought to have or did have acquired immune deficiency syndrome (AIDS).

Hugh Kaufman and the
Environmental Protection Agency

At the time of his whistleblowing in spring 1982, Hugh Kaufman was assistant to the director of the Hazardous Waste Site Control Division of the Environmental Protection Agency, serving under Rita M. Lavelle, the assistant administrator in charge of the Superfund program. Although not in the top echelon of EPA officials, Kaufman had been a career professional with the agency since 1971 and was an influential employee. Despite his modest formal position, he had developed a wide network of contacts outside the agency, particularly in the press and in Congress. He described himself as a whistleblower, although not a typical one, and as someone who knew how to "use the democratic process to affect the issues" (Kaufman 1989).

In his capacity as the EPA's chief toxic waste investigator during the 1970s, Kaufman had blown the whistle on the Carter administration's handling of hazardous-waste policy. Eventually he provided data to Congress on a number of hazardous-waste sites nationwide (including Love Canal), testified before congressional committees on the issue in 1978 and 1979, and helped create the political climate that made possible the adoption in 1980 of the Superfund program. That program established a $1.6 billion fund from which the EPA could draw to clean up dangerous waste dumps. Kaufman's actions in the late 1970s alerted him to the policy influence that could be associated with an "obvious strategy" of whistleblowing, which he would choose again under the Reagan administration (Kaufman 1989).

In the early 1980s the Reagan administration was determined to redirect environmental policy and to reduce what it viewed as excessively costly and burdensome federal regulation. In particular, it hoped to cut the EPA staff and operating budget by almost 50 percent despite new legislation that added greatly to the agency's workload (Vig and Kraft 1984). Not surprisingly, critics complained that the EPA was being virtually dismantled under its new administrator, Anne M. Gorsuch (later Burford). Critics were especially vocal about a slowdown in enforcement of hazardous-waste site cleanup, a popular program in the early stages of implementation. Kaufman's own job was not threatened by the general EPA cutbacks because the Superfund program was one of the few growth areas in the agency.

By March 1982, Hugh Kaufman began blowing the whistle once again. He appeared before several congressional committees, including a hearing on reauthorization of the Resource Conservation and Recovery Act (RCRA) of 1976, the nation's major hazardous-waste policy, and he gave frequent interviews to journalists. He charged the Reagan EPA with jeopardizing the public's health by failing to enforce hazardous-waste and toxic-chemical laws, arranging "sweetheart deals" with polluters, and allowing partisan politics to affect the program (House of Representatives 1982; Shabecoff 1982a, 1983). These charges were repeated in an interview on CBS's *60 Minutes* on April 24, 1982, which because of its vast audience, dramatically raised the political stakes for the administration.

Other EPA employees were making similar accusations to the press and before congressional committees concerning EPA mismanagement and failure to enforce the law (Burnham 1983). However, Kaufman was the most active and visible of EPA whistleblowers. This was no accident; he had a clear plan for achieving policy impact, and as part of it he tried to identify "pressure points for change." He also took advantage of windows of opportunity, asserting that "timing is everything" in trying to bring attention to agency abuses in the press and on Capitol Hill.

As is almost always the case with whistleblowers, Kaufman experienced reprisals, but he was successful in deflecting efforts to silence him. Even before the *60 Minutes* interview, he had been stripped of administrative responsibilities, his workload was increased with what he termed "meaningless paperwork," and he was harassed and investigated by the EPA (Shabecoff 1982a; Kaufman 1989). As many as fifteen EPA employees were involved in the investigation to try to find grounds to dismiss and/or intimidate Kaufman (Burnham 1982a). In response, he used what he terms an "offensive and defensive strategy" to maintain his influence and security; he appealed to his supervisor in the EPA, filed a formal complaint with the Department of Labor, and went to the media. Ultimately he was successful in reaching a settlement through the Department of Labor, in February 1983, amid a raging controversy over the Superfund program (Shabecoff 1983; Burnham 1982b).[1] The EPA was ordered to refrain from taking any steps to prevent Kaufman from criticizing the agency, which allowed him to engage in further acts of whistleblowing.

As already explained, there are three dimensions of policy impact to be examined: the shaping of the policy agenda, the altering of bureaucratic processes, and the changing of substantive policy. Each of these dimensions of the Kaufman case is examined in turn.

The Policy Agenda

The heart of Kaufman's accusations was that the agency was failing to comply with environmental law on toxic and hazardous chemicals, probably, as Kraft and Vig suggest, a direct consequence of the Reagan administration's agenda for environmental deregulation (1984). The specific "wrongdoing" in this case centered on the charge that Burford and Lavelle were not spending Superfund money as called for in the law and were misusing or misdirecting program funds. Kaufman's allegations related to the EPA's use of "enforcement-sensitive documents" that were protected by the president's use of executive privilege. But Kaufman and some members of Congress believed that some of these documents showed potentially criminal activity. Hence Kaufman's focus was not merely on preferred policy alternatives but on violations of law. Because the controversy concerned hazardous chemicals, his accusations were likely to gain media and congressional attention. There had been sustained publicity over Love Canal and other chemical dump sites at the time the Superfund program was enacted in 1980, and the public was increasingly concerned about the risks of toxic chemicals and hazardous waste.

Kaufman took little for granted in designing his "strategy" of whistleblowing. He tried to maximize impact on the policy agenda by developing, in association with Representatives James Scheuer and Mike Synar, a "carefully orchestrated plan" for exposing EPA abuses. Scheuer and Synar asked Kaufman to collect pertinent EPA documents and deliver them to their subcommittees after his settlement with the EPA over its illegal investigation of him was final, which occurred on February 14, 1983 (Kaufman 1989). At that time, Kaufman was sufficiently protected from agency reprisals that he felt he could criticize the EPA openly. Along with Scheuer and Synar, he arranged for news coverage of the transmittal of those documents. A *New York Times* article on February 17, 1983, included a photograph showing Kaufman seated between Scheuer and Synar, with a caption saying he was "delivering a box of documents" to them. The subcommittee chairmen told the *Times* reporter that the documents indicated "potential wrongdoing" at the agency, and they promised to hold hearings on them (Maitland 1983).

Kaufman's action had the effect he and his congressional allies hoped for. The Reagan White House, unsure of what documents Congress had in its possession, and reportedly nervous about possible criminal charges, dropped its claim of executive privilege for EPA documents. At a presidential news conference held the same day that Kaufman delivered the documents to Congress, President Reagan said he would "never invoke executive privilege to cover up wrongdoing," and he pledged cooperation with Congress in its investigation of the agency as well as "a complete investigation" by the Justice Department of all charges made (Maitland 1983). This White House decision set in motion Anne Burford's resignation as EPA administrator a month later and the subsequent transformation, with wholesale replacement of EPA's top leadership. The ultimate effect on the agency's environmental policy agenda was substantial. Crucial to these developments was the fact that five House subcommittees (including Scheuer's and Synar's) and one Senate committee were investigating EPA implementation of hazardous-waste laws and Burford's leadership of the agency.

Kaufman's impact on the policy agenda was made possible through his active collaboration with Scheuer and Synar, whose well-publicized subcommittee investigations spurred broader congressional scrutiny of the EPA, including a thorough examination by Representative John Dingell's influential Oversight and Investigations Subcommittee (Davis 1983). A favorable political climate, including public concern over hazardous waste, extensive media coverage of EPA abuses and internal turmoil, and congressional displeasure with Reagan's environmental policies, helped to make his success possible.

Bureaucratic Procedures

Prior to the arrival of the Reagan administration, the EPA was widely credited with being one of the most professional, competent, and stable federal agencies. To further its new environmental agenda, however, the administration believed it had to mount a direct challenge to career EPA personnel it considered to be unsympathetic to Reagan's new policy goals (Davies 1984). Given these conditions, opposition by career staff such as Hugh Kaufman was to be expected, and there was an increased chance that whistleblowing could have an impact on EPA personnel and procedures.

The linkage between Kaufman's whistleblowing and changes within the EPA was strengthened by the fallout from the agency's probe of Kaufman's activities. As noted, the EPA began an investigation of Kaufman in an effort to silence him, but the strategy backfired. Kaufman charged, before another House subcommittee, that EPA officials were harassing him and were trying to have him fired to end criticism of the hazardous-waste program. These accusations were examined by at least four House subcommittees in July 1982. In one case, Representative Scheuer threatened to bring perjury charges against Lavelle for having denied under oath that she ordered an investigation of Kaufman. By early February 1983, Lavelle was fired by the White

House in an effort to quell the growing controversy, and with assurances offered by Scheuer that he would drop the charges. Lavelle's effort to silence Kaufman contributed to her dismissal. Kaufman himself leaked a memo from Lavelle's office that criticized EPA general counsel Robert Perry for alienating the "primary constituency of this Administration, the business community." The memo was given to David Burnham of the *New York Times*, and is often cited as the decisive factor in Lavelle's firing.[2]

Lavelle's dismissal began a sweeping set of high-level personnel changes at the agency. Kaufman's role in bringing about these changes was clearly significant, not only in leaking critical memos to the press, but in becoming the subject of an investigation that in turn expanded the issue of mismanagement at the EPA. Indeed, *New York Times* writer Stuart Taylor listed EPA investigation and surveillance of Kaufman, among other evidence of the use of political "hit lists" within the agency, as one of the "four issues" central to the larger EPA controversy (Taylor 1983b). Within a few months, these events of spring 1983 led to a number of crucial and long-lasting changes within the EPA, particularly in agency personnel and leadership.

By 1982, extensive budget cuts and the antienvironmental posture of the Reagan administration had created dismal morale at the EPA. According to one report in early 1982, dissidents within the agency were said to "leak virtually every budget draft and controversial memo to the press and to a growing number of [Burford's] critics in Congress" (Henry 1982). Burford complained at the height of the controversy in 1983 that "it's not easy to run an agency when the whole work force is either under subpoena or at the Xerox machine" (Dowd 1983: 16). That climate changed significantly when she was forced out of office in March 1983, along with nearly two dozen other top EPA officials. She was replaced by former EPA administrator William Ruckelshaus, who, in his brief tenure, brought to the agency a new team of competent, experienced, and professional policy officials and helped to restore some degree of staff morale and integrity.

Beyond these impacts on the agency's personnel and leadership, Kaufman's actions stimulated Congress to intervene in EPA agency rules resulting in changed procedures. In 1984, Congress revised the 1976 RCRA and imposed on the agency much more stringent standards and deadlines. They cut back sharply on discretionary power previously granted to the EPA. In addition, there were changes in administrative style and policy implementation. EPA decisionmaking from 1983 to

1988 was less confrontational than under Burford and, to some extent at least, policy became more moderate; there were fewer efforts to delay or weaken new regulations, and policy implementation improved (Vig and Kraft 1984: 363–366; Bowman 1988; Wood 1988). These patterns continued under Lee Thomas, who took over as EPA administrator after Ruckelshaus departed in January 1985. They were still evident in 1989, when President George H. W. Bush named a prominent environmentalist, William Reilly, to head the agency.

Thus, Hugh Kaufman's influence on the EPA in 1983 was considerable. He stimulated media coverage of personnel and other abuses that induced congressional oversight hearings, and eventually White House intervention that replaced the top leadership at the agency. It is unlikely that Ruckelshaus would have been invited back to the agency had Kaufman and others not been so effective in criticizing the EPA under Burford. Although such an impact is inherently difficult to document, at least one close observer of the EPA controversies offered an assessment of Kaufman's role. *New York Times* correspondent David Burnham in 1986 compared Kaufman to two prominent whistleblowers, Ernest Fitzgerald and Frank Serpico, and said "you can attribute the uncovering of EPA's inactivity [on toxic waste] and Rita Lavelle's misconduct to Hugh Kaufman as much as anyone else" (*Washington Monthly* 1986). Kaufman himself describes his influence as that of a "catalyst" whose actions brought about such changes within the EPA in part because the "timing was right" and he was in a "linchpin" position (Kaufman 1989). In terms of the original hypothesis, Kaufman's personal characteristics (his status in the EPA and especially his political skills), the saliency of hazardous-waste issues, and the favorable political environment of 1983 created conditions highly conducive to influence personnel and procedural changes through his act of whistleblowing.

Public Policy

Finally, evidence suggests that Hugh Kaufman also had an impact on hazardous-waste policy itself. Congressional investigation of the multifaceted scandal at EPA reached a peak in late 1982 and early 1983, and it was front-page news in the nation's press when Anne Burford became the first cabinet-level official ever to be cited for contempt by the House of Representatives; the citation was prompted, as already described, by her refusal, on presidential orders, to turn over subpoenaed EPA documents on management of the Superfund program

(Shabecoff 1982b). The immediate dispute over the documents was settled when the Justice Department dropped its claim of executive privilege and gave the House Public Works Committee's investigating subcommittee access to the EPA documents in question. That was hardly
likely to be the end of the story, however, given the prominence of the
issues and congressional interest in revising environmental statutes to
prevent the kinds of administrative abuses widely criticized during
Burford's tenure at the agency.

Accusations against Lavelle, Burford, and others in the EPA were
made at a time of growing public concern about hazardous chemicals,
and just after congressional passage of the Superfund Act in 1980. They
also occurred as the EPA was completing action on comprehensive regulations to enforce the other major hazardous-waste law, the RCRA of
1976. Moreover, Congress (at least the House, with its Democratic
majority) was anxious to protect and strengthen a number of major
environmental policies to counteract Reagan administration efforts to
weaken them. Hugh Kaufman arrived at an opportune moment.

Given these conditions, Kaufman clearly played a role similar to
the policy entrepreneur (Kingdon 1995). As a whistleblower making
specific charges of illegal conduct, he added to the visibility of hazardous-waste policy issues and the momentum of EPA investigations on
the Hill, and he spurred Congress to examine the adequacy of policy at
that time. In 1984, Congress did impose stricter standards, in effect saying that it didn't trust the Reagan EPA to administer the law without
imposing such restrictions. Similarly, Congress expanded the Superfund
program in 1986, greatly increasing authorizations (to nearly $9 billion
over a five-year period) and adding significant new requirements for
public notification of chemical risks and for cleaning up abandoned
waste sites. Neither the case nor the hypothesis allows us to say Hugh
Kaufman alone was responsible for these changes. But we can say that
he played a pivotal role in 1982 and 1983, affecting the timing of key
decisions, and thereby increasing the likelihood that significant policy
change would occur.

Hal Freeman and the Office for Civil Rights

Hal Freeman had been regional manager for two years in the San
Francisco Office for Civil Rights (OCR), in the U.S. Department of
Health and Human Services (HHS), when he resigned in protest over

OCR policy regarding discrimination against persons with AIDS or AIDS-related conditions, or persons who were perceived as having such a condition (Freeman 1986b). His issue was specific and it was feasible to address. In his resignation letter to Betty Lou Dotson, a Reagan appointee and then director of OCR, Freeman argued that people with AIDS, and those thought to have AIDS, were protected by the Section 504 regulations of the Vocational Rehabilitation Act of 1973, which prohibits discrimination on the basis of handicap. Because of the emergency nature of the AIDS epidemic, he called for prompt action by OCR and he alluded to the Reagan administration's general record of nonenforcement (Freeman 1986b).

It was just a few months earlier that his San Francisco office had received OCR's first AIDS-related case from Philip Monfette, a jail medical technician (Monfette 1985). When in accordance with OCR instructions, Freeman had contacted headquarters, Dotson's assistant deemed the complaint "low priority," doubted that OCR had jurisdiction (Freeman 1985), and referred the complaint to the Department of Justice (Hood 1986a). By February, the Department of Justice had kicked the case back to OCR (Oneglia 1986), where headquarters kept administrative control of the cases (Dotson 1986); without a clear policy, regional offices were unable to respond to complaints or public inquiries (Graff 1986; Adams 1986b; Freeman 1986a).

Freeman had status and visibility because of his position as OCR manager for a four-state region and his resignation almost immediately became public knowledge and helped focus public attention on the issue. Copies of his resignation letter circulated throughout OCR, ripples ran through the civil-rights community, Freeman's phone was ringing off the hook, and press coverage and congressional inquiries followed (Macpherson 1989).

Freeman's resignation and the stories in major newspapers that publicized it had significant impact (Cimons 1986; Mathews 1986; Schilts 1986; "HHS Executive Quits" 1986). When he blew the whistle on the AIDS-related civil-rights issue, by raising questions about OCR's policy of general nonenforcement, Freeman also got the attention of the more traditional civil-rights organizations as well as the newer gay and AIDS-connected groups. But even more important was Freeman's success in congressional networking. Many congressional Democrats were not happy with the Reagan record on civil rights. The resignation provoked a critical response, especially from California legislators. Representative Henry Waxman (D-CA), chair of the House Energy and

Commerce Subcommittee on Health and the Environment, spoke forcefully about his concern over the issue; Representative Ted Weiss (D-
NY), chair of the Government Operations Subcommittee on
Intergovernmental Relations and Human Resources, promised hearings
("HHS Official Quits" 1986); and Senator Alan Cranston (D-CA) sent a
detailed letter to the secretary of Health and Human Services, Otis
Bowen, expressing his "great disappointment" in the way OCR was
handling AIDS-related cases. In his letter, Cranston specifically referred
to Freeman's resignation letter and "as a principal Senate author" of the
504 regulations, Cranston called "preposterous" the interpretation that
"AIDS . . . is not an impairment under Section 504" (Cranston
1986).

Meanwhile, Representative Mervyn Dymally (D-CA) was working
behind the scenes, assisted by an OCR employee, Jim Fukumoto, who
since 1984 had been detailed to Congress as a legislative fellow by a
special Office of Personnel Management HHS program. With
Fukumoto's help, in early March, Dymally wrote strong letters to Ted
Weiss and Henry Waxman about his concern about a possible breach of
law, urging his colleagues to continue to exercise their oversight
responsibilities (Dymally 1986a, 1986b).

One option Freeman had was to blow the whistle and continue to
work for OCR. However, because he knew there would be reprisals if
he publicly protested and continued to work in that office, he decided to
resign (Macpherson 1989). A whistleblower who resigns may also experience reprisals, but Freeman was unconcerned for two reasons: he was
not only leaving government employment altogether, but he was also
entering a new field (the private practice of psychology) where team
play and loyalty to an organization were not as important.

The Policy Agenda

What effect did Freeman's public resignation have in changing the policy against which he protested? Before he acted, the issue of civil-rights
protections for people with AIDS or HIV and for people suspected of
having AIDS or HIV was not widely discussed or publicly debated in
the media and in Congress. Thus, as we have seen, Freeman had a clear
impact on the policy agenda. "There was no story until the resignation,"
said insider Jim Fukumoto (1989). Freeman stimulated public discussion and group action, especially among civil-rights advocates, which
included traditional groups such as the National Association for the
Advancement of Colored People (NAACP) (McClure 1986) as well as

gay activists, whose work to get local antidiscrimination laws passed in cities and counties was fueled by the resignation. Freeman got instant media coverage with his resignation, but he also helped put the issue on the agenda for many affirmative-action and equal-opportunity officers who flooded the OCR regional office with inquiries (Robertson 1989). The resignation in protest was also a perfect hook to help some members of Congress set a congressional agenda that would embarrass the Reagan administration on its civil-rights record. Freeman would be a star witness at congressional hearings six months later. Thus, while it was not a highly salient issue for the general public, the question of whether people with AIDS or those thought to have AIDS were protected from discrimination became a part of many social and governmental agendas at this time because of Hal Freeman's public resignation.

Bureaucratic Procedures

What impact did Freeman's resignation have on the very practices and procedures he could not change as regional manager? It is hard to measure such an impact because many of the procedures and policies might have been changed in due course as a result of other political and legal pressures. Nevertheless, all those interviewed for this case agree that this resignation, by exposing OCR the way it did, "broke the dam" and started a flood of procedural changes that could not be stopped.

To begin with, less than one week after the Freeman resignation, each region, at headquarters' request, designated a staff person to coordinate the processing of AIDS complaints (Hood 1986b). It was a step toward preparing for AIDS-related cases but also represented a move by headquarters, as one anonymous informant put it, to "micromanage" the processing of the cases with daily reporting requirements (Anonymous 1989). July 1986 procedural guidelines, and those prepared by headquarters in November 1986, required that the regions forward to Washington, on a tight schedule, information on their cases and an investigative plan for headquarters' approval because "administrative control of AIDS/ARC cases is at the headquarters level" (Apodaca 1986; Office for Civil Rights 1986).

As a result of Freeman's actions, organizational behavior in Region IX (San Francisco) changed in another way. The office began an extensive outreach program. While the administration kept tight control of the region's complaint procedures and skirted the issue of just what OCR's AIDS policy was, the Region IX office under its new manager, Virginia Apodaca, mounted a mailing to all AIDS service groups within the region that were listed with the Center for Disease Control. By June 1986, a Region IX fact sheet had been sent to 900 groups. By November 1986, the mailing had expanded to state antidiscrimination agencies and municipalities as well as lawyers' groups, inviting them to refer discrimination cases to OCR. Mailings also went to "gay" periodicals, and the fact sheet was made available in Chinese, Spanish, and Tagalog. The June fact sheet mailing boldly invited persons with AIDS or related conditions who believed they had been discriminated against on the basis of handicap to file a complaint with OCR in HHS because of the protections of Section 504 of the Rehabilitation Act of 1973 (Department of Health and Human Services, Region IX, 1986).

According to Apodaca, Freeman's resignation made it "more possible to do the mailing. It might have been ignored before; it was now an issue" (Apodaca 1989). Another source suggested that headquarters could not prevent the provocative mailing because OCR was now so exposed to public attention and congressional scrutiny on the issue that "clamping down" would represent proof that OCR was not enforcing the law (Anonymous 1989). In every major city, there were AIDS-related foundations and gay organizations that cooperated by doing supplementary mailings and networking to communicate the "policy" (Apodaca 1986). Thus Freeman's whistleblowing directly affected the regional office's action and its action helped further mobilize organized interests. Ironically, Betty Lou Dotson, director of OCR, presented Apodaca with an award for her AIDS outreach activities in October 1986 at a meeting of all the regional managers.

Nevertheless, HHS still did not have an "official" policy on discrimination and AIDS, and so, in March, the HHS general counsel asked the Justice Department to clarify OCR's responsibilities toward people with AIDS or those thought to have AIDS. Apodaca suggested that going to the Justice Department for policy was "unprecedented" and a delaying tactic, noting that there was "sufficient legal talent in HHS to make the determination" (1986).

In response to the request, Stewart Oneglia, in the Justice Department's Civil Rights Division, prepared an opinion consistent with the opinions of the mostly career civil-service attorneys in his section. It was leaked to the press and published in the *New York Times* on June 8, 1986. It argued that people with AIDS are handicapped and entitled to protection (Abramson 1986: 15; Pear 1986). The *New York Times* reported that this was the Department of Justice's "final position on the issue" and that "senior officials said there was little disagreement within the department" (Pear 1986).

Nothing could have been further from the truth. Two weeks later, Assistant Attorney General Charles Cooper issued the Justice Department's "official" opinion and "it bore almost no resemblance" to Oneglia's draft. Cooper argued that "an immune carrier does not have a physical or mental impairment" (handicap) and that while employers cannot discriminate against a person because he has AIDS, they can discriminate "based on concern about contagiousness" (Abramson 1986: 15). According to two sources, the Cooper document was leaked to the *New York Times* so that it could appear in the Sunday edition to get the most publicity possible, by someone who would not have done it had it not been for Freeman's resignation. The *New York Times* of July 15 headlined the story, "Justice Department Supports Discrimination Based on Fear of Contagion," and the *Wall Street Journal* cited widespread opposition to Cooper's policy within the business community (Abramson 1986: 15–16). Indeed, HHS now had an official opinion; it was not very popular in the press and it was not long-lasting. Both the Supreme Court and Congress rejected the interpretation.

Public Policy

The Supreme Court rejected Cooper's interpretation in *School Board of Nassau County v. Arline*, a case involving a person with a contagious disease, tuberculosis, who was discharged from a tenured teaching position because of a fear by the school board that she would threaten the health of students and colleagues. On July 14, 1986, the solicitor general used the Cooper argument and reasoned that "Arline was discharged not because of her disability but because of her infection. . . . The mere 'belief that an individual is contagious—whether reasonable or not,' was sufficient to absolve the school board of discrimination" (Cook 1987: 17).

The majority of the Supreme Court rejected this perspective, and Justice William Brennan wrote the opinion, which argued that the Section 504 regulation protects individuals from prejudice (Barnes and Frankfurt 1987: 6). It is unlikely that Freeman, the whistleblower, affected very directly the outcome of a judicial case that had to do with a black schoolteacher with tuberculosis who was fired in 1979. However, his resignation did affect what Congress did during the sum-

mer of 1986. The Intergovernmental Relations and Human Resources
Subcommittee hearings, promised by Representative Ted Weiss, were
held on August 6 and 7, 1986. Not only did Freeman's resignation stimulate the hearings, his impact was felt in two other ways: through the
credibility of his presentation as one of the committee's "star" witnesses
and through the stimulation his resignation gave to others to cooperate
with the oversight investigation.

As a former regional manager who no longer had his job to protect,
Freeman was quoted extensively in the committee's report. Like
Kaufman, Freeman's personal characteristics (his status and skills)
made him an especially effective whistleblower. Conditions within the
agency also favored change; many staffers disagreed with the Reagan
policy and Freeman's resignation spurred OCR staff in headquarters to
cooperate with the committee. One dramatic case was Pat Hoffman,
special assistant to the deputy director, who admitted that "Hal set the
stage for me to go to the committee" (Hoffman 1989).

Apparently, Betty Lou Dotson, director of OCR, had traveled
extensively "on taxpayers' money"—126 trips to thirty-eight U.S. cities
and nine foreign countries at a cost of $86,858 during her first five
years as director. She also ran up $6,840 in taxi fares on her domestic
trips (Kurtz 1986, 1987; Davidson 1986). Hoffman had reported this to
the inspector general in 1982, but nothing was done because Dotson
was a political appointee. In April 1986, Hoffman leaked information
on Dotson's travel vouchers to the Weiss subcommittee. Hoffman vol-
unteered that "Hal's resignation gave me the courage to do what I did"
(1989). Her anonymity was protected by the committee until it directed
the General Accounting Office to investigate the travel abuses and GAO
"blew Hoffman's cover." That's when she realized there were at least
fifteen others in the office who were primed to do something or who
were already cooperating with the investigation. They had revealed
themselves to Hoffman because her whistleblowing had been exposed.
All this occurred, Hoffman said, because Freeman had resigned (1989).
Said another informant, "Hal made people bolder." People were "fueled
by Hal's resignation." He had "sacrificed his career, people were asked
to sacrifice and risk" (Anonymous 1989). Jim Fukumoto also characterized Freeman's unique impact on events: "Hal catalyzed the internal
workings [of OCR], and something happened to someone who was not
controversial." Freeman "gave it momentum and credibility; no one had
faced [Dotson] down, resigned in protest" (Fukumoto 1989).

The publicity from the hearings hit the agency hard. It exposed its weak enforcement record where cases were "allowed to sit languishing at headquarters for policy formulation and determination which [was] never made," according to Representative Dymally, who was a witness at the hearings. OCR was described by the committee as "out of control" (Marlow 1986: 7). But even before the sound of the first gavel, the committee hearings affected substantive policy. The initial tangible policy fallout from the hearings occurred the night before the first committee session, when OCR issued its first decision on an AIDS discrimination case, filed in Atlanta. OCR found a hospital that had fired a nurse because he had AIDS, in violation of the 504 regulations (Hoffman 1989).

However, by far the biggest effect of the hearings was its impact on Dotson, who was forced to resign on March 13, 1987; the revelations about her travel abuses left her too vulnerable for the administration to keep her on. According to two informants, Dotson had been "getting her signals from the administration," which tried to protect her when she was attacked. In the beginning, the administration refused to honor requests from Congress that Justice or the inspector general investigate her. When she had to resign, the administration appointed her representative to the Bicentennial Commission on the Constitution in order to save her pension (Kurtz 1987).

Dotson's departure was more than a bureaucratic personnel change and had more than a symbolic effect; it directly affected civil-rights policy. It was no secret that Dotson was unsympathetic toward people with AIDS. According to sources, she was overheard to have said, "I'm not going to do something which gives these people an aura of dignity." She was also overheard asking her assistant "how she could avoid taking complaints from those people." The hearings and then her departure "opened things up so we could do our jobs again" (Hoffman 1989).

On April 16, 1987, the House Committee on Government Operations released the Weiss subcommittee report. It accused OCR of failing to do its job, of delaying cases, and of allowing discrimination to continue (House of Representatives 1987; Rich 1987). No separate mention was made of AIDS discrimination cases because OCR AIDS policy and OCR bureaucratic procedures had already been changed. Many of the regions were receiving AIDS-related cases, regional representatives had been trained in AIDS-related issues, and cases were being handled expeditiously with time frames that gave them priority status.

One month after the House report, Hal Freeman found out he had

AIDS. A year later, in August 1988, in a massive mailing, Audry Morton, the new OCR director, gave notice to 100,000 HHS recipients across the country that "persons who have or are perceived as having AIDS or AIDS-related conditions . . . may not be discriminated against under any federally assisted program or activity." By September 1988, the office of the assistant attorney general released a memorandum reversing the Cooper opinion (Kmiec 1988).

But Hal Freeman had died two months earlier. A week after his death, Representative Dymally entered Freeman's resignation letter into the Congressional Record, prefaced by a statement crediting him with influencing public debate over protection of people with AIDS and the enforcement of civil-rights laws. Pat Hoffman, in OCR headquarters, prepared a patch for the national AIDS quilt. It included the HHS seal and a quote from Freeman's resignation letter: "My greater allegiance is to my conscience and to my commitment to eliminate bigotry in all its forms."

Comparison of the Cases

These two cases demonstrate bureaucratic whistleblowing that had an important impact on public policy. In each case the data indicate a substantial effect on the policy agenda, agency procedures, and substantive policy. But these are unusual cases. The prevailing pattern is that whistleblowing has no such policy impact (Truelson 1986; Soeken and Soeken 1987). These cases of successful whistleblowing are instructive precisely because they are exceptions to the pattern. The policy impact found here suggests conditions that may determine whether and to what extent such impacts are likely in other cases. The analytic framework posits that three sets of variables will condition policy impact: the characteristics of the whistleblower (status, credibility, and political skills), the characteristics of the issue (saliency, specificity, and feasibility of corrective action), and the political environment (public opinion, group activity, media coverage, and legislative receptivity to change). A comparison of the two cases along these dimensions is instructive to understanding whistleblowing and policy change.

The cases illustrate how the status, credibility, and political skills of whistleblowers can determine both the range of their options and the extent of impact they can have. It appears that the higher the status and the greater the credibility and political skills of the whistleblower, the greater is the probability of policy impact. Kaufman was an experienced and politically astute mid-level official at the EPA who had extensive knowledge of the hazardous-waste control program, a wide network of contacts in the press and on Capitol Hill, a record of successful whistle-blowing, and a newly protected status in the agency. These characteristics enabled him to influence the environmental policy agenda at a critical time in the early 1980s, contribute significantly to important shifts in EPA personnel and procedures in 1983 and later years, and shape revisions in federal hazardous-waste policy adopted by Congress in 1984 and 1986.

Similarly, Freeman was the OCR regional manager of a four-state area who had abundant political and media contacts, credibility stemming from his expertise and experience, and who was willing to resign in protest to further his goals of policy change. These attributes contributed greatly to his ability to expand the civil-rights agenda to include protection in cases involving AIDS, to affect personnel and procedures within OCR, and to shape the development of new public policy in this area.

These cases also demonstrate how issue characteristics can affect a whistleblower's chances of success. I hypothesize that the more salient, specific, and administratively feasible the change demanded by the whistleblower, the more likely he or she is to succeed. Freeman's issue was quite specific: to apply antidiscrimination laws to people with AIDS and those thought to have AIDS, and his activities occurred at a time when concern over AIDS was growing appreciably both in the medical community and among the general public. As the saliency of such issues increases, there is more incentive for journalists and politicians to become involved, and whistleblowing becomes similar to what Gormley (1989) describes as catalytic controls on bureaucracy.

Kaufman's issue was broader, but still relatively specific: he wanted better public protection from hazardous wastes and thus stronger enforcement of RCRA and the Superfund law. Moreover, like Freeman's campaign for extending civil-rights protection, Kaufman's actions occurred at a time of rising issue saliency; the public was increasingly worried about toxic chemicals and hazardous wastes, and the Reagan administration's environmental policies, including program cutbacks and reduced enforcement, were widely publicized. Both Freeman and Kaufman championed issues of concern to constituents served by their agencies, which also made their success more likely. Finally, they called for manageable changes that affected one agency or that required revisions in the law, a change in its interpretation, or increased funds, none of which was unfeasible at the time. Their goals were also consistent with the missions of their agencies.

Perhaps the most essential factor for successful policy impact is a favorable political environment. By definition, whistleblowers do not bring about change from within the agency, but go outside the organization to have impact. Their success depends as much on the interest, commitment, and actions of others as it does on their own skills or the merits of their arguments. I hypothesize that the more supportive the political environment is during whistleblowing, the greater the probability of policy impact.

As Kaufman himself hinted (1989), whistleblowers may act like policy entrepreneurs whose ability to stimulate others to take an interest in the issues and become involved, particularly journalists, interest group activists, and influential legislators, is important to the effects they have (Kingdon 1995). The nature and extent of the impact will depend on the incentives offered these external parties to pay attention to the issues and act on them. For these two cases, there was a supportive political environment; a Republican administration was confronted by a Democratic House of Representatives eager to challenge its conservative policy agenda. In addition, either public opinion clearly favored the policy change being advocated (especially notable in the environmental policy case) or effective advocacy coalitions were mobilized to further the changes (especially evident in the civil-rights case). These conditions provide strong incentives for the conduct of legislative oversight hearings (Aberbach 1979), which occurred in both cases. Congressional actions eventually led to important changes in the two agencies.

Tying It All Together

Conventional analyses of whistleblowing focus on individuals' acts of conscience, often ignoring the changes effected by whistleblowers. This chapter fills a gap by focusing on their policy impact and by exploring the factors that contribute to whistleblower success.

The two case studies chosen are of whistleblowers who helped to bring about significant changes in public policy. Data from the cases suggest strongly that whistleblowers can indeed have an impact on public policy under certain conditions. These conditions include characteristics of the whistleblowers themselves and of the issues they champion. Especially important is a supportive political environment: extensive and sympathetic media coverage, general public support and active support by politically influential groups, and strong interest on the part of legislators in a position to conduct oversight investigations and promote policy change. Let me suggest for further testing that the more these conditions are met, the greater the likelihood that policy impact will occur. By focusing on the consequences of whistleblowing, this chapter helps fill a gap in the existing literature (Elliston et al. 1985: 164–167; Bowman, Elliston, and Lockhart 1984) and ties whistleblowing to other mechanisms of bureaucratic accountability (Gormley 1989; Gruber 1987).

The study of whistleblower impact is a crucial part of the study of whistleblowing. While the stories of individuals fighting against large and seemingly irresponsible bureaucracies are dramatic and often poignant, the more important story may be the long-term policy changes effected by their personal crusades.

The focus of the next chapter will be on one such case. Barbara Moulton was a whistleblower in the Food and Drug Administration in the early 1960s. While almost always in the background, Moulton had a major and lasting impact on her agency's policy and mission. Although her name may not be recognized, many will be familiar with her story.

Notes

Portions of this chapter are drawn from "Bureaucratic Whistleblowing and Policy Change," *Western Political Quarterly* 43, no. 4 (December 1990), pp. 849–874. Reprinted by permission of the University of Utah. The article was coauthored with Michael Kraft from the University of Wisconsin at Green Bay. I am grateful to Professor Kraft for his important contributions, much of which I have used in this chapter with his permission.

1. The Labor Department was investigating the case because the Superfund law contains a provision that protects the rights of federal officials to publicly criticize government actions related to the protection of the environment. (A discussion of this and other such area-specific whistleblower protection is described in Chapter 5.) In this case, the Labor Department ruled that the EPA had wrongfully investigated Kaufman's activities and sought to "silence the communication of ideas." As part of the settlement with the EPA, the agency dropped all pending actions against Kaufman.

2. It seems that one of Kaufman's "operatives" in the agency pulled the Lavelle memo off a computer disk belonging to one of her aides, who was the author. Kaufman sent it on to Burnham. When Burnham called an EPA official

to ask about it, the official notified Burford of its existence. The memo gave her the opportunity to fire Lavelle for undermining a fellow member of the EPA team and then lying about it. On February 4, 1983, Burford asked Lavelle to resign and she refused. President Reagan fired her two days later (Bonner 1983b).

4

The Whistleblower's Impact
on the Agency

What effects do whistleblowers have on their own agencies? Curiously, short-term effects are often quite negative. In some instances, whistleblowers can weaken an organization's chain of command, pose a threat to its effectiveness, unsettle employees' confidence in their ability to use discretion, and create a sense of unpredictability.

When whistleblowers succeed in making the public aware of agency wrongdoing, malfeasance, corruption, or fraud, the news is bound to embarrass the agency. In fact, the publicity from whistleblowing might also cause financial losses for the agency, a reduction in public support, increased management turnover, and sometimes loss of cohesion within the organization (Micelli and Near 1992). This is indeed what happened to the Internal Revenue Service after the well-publicized congressional testimony of whistleblowers in 1997 and 1998 (Johnston 1999a–d, 2000a, 2000b).

While all these short-term negative consequences may result from the public exposure, whistleblowers can, of course, have immediate beneficial effects on agencies because they address the problem of dangerous practices or corruption. In fact, it has been suggested that whistleblowers also benefit the wider society by helping to eliminate and control individual and organizational misconduct (Miethe 1999: 83).[1]

The immediate beneficial effects of whistleblowers are especially apparent in high-stakes areas of public health and safety because of the substantial potential dangers posed. Miceli and Near point to nuclear power plants, pharmaceutical firms, and automobile manufacturers as places where decisions can have "consequences that would preserve

75

life or its quality." They suggest that in these organizations, which operate daily with the threat of a catastrophe, "in the event of mistakes" whistleblowing could be a kind of early alarm system (Miceli and Near 1992: 11). Of course, we can add to their life/death list many other arenas where this is also so, such as airline travel, toxic waste, and the safety and purity of our air, water, and food. Clearly, since September 11, 2001, the public may also be more appreciative of any early alarm systems that may help to protect against a potential terrorist threat.

The nuclear power industry, one of the high-stakes areas, is the home to many important whistleblowing efforts. Insider information has made a significant difference there in protecting the public and alerting Congress and other policymakers to serious dangers (Government Accountability Project 1997: 5–7). Nowhere was this more evident than at the Hanford Atomic Reservation.

The Hanford Site

"Hanford was to plutonium what Pittsburgh was to steel. And almost everything about it was top secret" (Lynch 1999b). Located in Richland, Washington, in the central part of the state, Hanford is a 560-square-mile, fifty-year-old nuclear weapons complex and is currently the Department of Energy's biggest environmental problem. At least two-thirds of the United States' defense wastes are being stored there. In fact, some call it "the most polluted place in the Western world" (D'Antonio 1993: 1).

Hanford was one of the first sites used by the Manhattan Project in World War II. A cluster of three cities—Richland, Pasco, and Kennewick—was formed around the site in the 1940s, "with their fortunes tied literally to a bomb" (Wade 1998).

Hanford was the source of plutonium used to make the atomic bomb dropped on Nagasaki, Japan, in 1945. After World War II, Hanford's legacy was linked to the development of nuclear weapons during the Cold War (House of Representatives 1993: 5). And now, because of the massive challenge of cleanup and decontamination, Hanford has become, according to Senator Frank Murkowski, (R-AL), "the largest civil works project in the history of mankind" (Senate 1995: 1).

The Hanford Atomic Reservation, currently referred to as the

"Hanford Site," was a "top secret government facility" (D'Antonio 1993: 1). Although it has not produced plutonium since 1987, Hanford continues to be a nuclear storage site. "About 54 million gallons of radioactive waste, in liquid, sludge and dried salt forms, is stored at Hanford in 177 underground tanks." Each storage tank is as large as the dome of the U.S. Capitol building in Washington, D.C. (House of Representatives 1993: 22). One hundred and forty-nine of the tanks "are made of a single shell of steel, and about 68 had leaked, releasing about 900,000 gallons into the soil. The oldest tanks are more than 50 years old, and all the single-shell tanks are expected to leak eventually" (Wald 1998).

"In addition to the stored wastes, there is an estimated 100 square miles of contaminated groundwater beneath the site, the result of hundreds of billions of gallons of radioactive water dumped directly into the ground over the years" (Murphy 2000b). By the year 2000, surveys found tritium (a substance known to cause birth defects) "at concentrations 90 times the Federal drinking water standard" in well-water that was dangerously close (only three and a half miles) to the Columbia River.

Contamination of the Columbia River would represent an ecological catastrophe. It is a waterway that "irrigates 1 million acres of prime farmland in two states and nurtures 80% of the fall chinook salmon harvested in Alaska and British Columbia" (Murphy 2000b).

The U.S. Department of Energy (DOE), which was responsible for Hanford, had unfortunately not been facing up to and solving this as well as other contamination problems at the site. In 1998, Senator Ron Wyden (D-OR) accused the department of "sticking its head in the contaminated sand, for years, years" (Wald 1998). By 1999, DOE, aided by dozens of private companies and with "input from the state," was overseeing a cleanup that employed 14,000 workers and cost $1.5 billion a year. Nevertheless, according to reporter Jim Lynch of the *Seattle Times Magazine*, and many other informed observers, these efforts were barely addressing the contamination that resulted from years of neglect. A newspaper columnist even suggested that "Hanford glows like a Budweiser sign" (Lynch 1999b).

The high-stakes threat and the complexity of the mess made Hanford a special case. Because assessment and cleanup methods were not only expensive but also new and sometimes untried, and there were no clear cleanup standards (House of Representatives 1993: 24), mistakes could be, and were made, worsening Hanford's contamination problem. The complexity of the contamination and serious "gaps in knowledge," according to *New York Times* reporter Matthew L. Wald, exacerbated the situation.[2]

Hanford's environmental condition was "so bizarre and severe it made other Superfund cleanup sites look like driveway oil spills" (Lynch 1999b) and yet the DOE seemed to be dragging its feet. The federal agency was slow to respond to the concerns of the Washington State Department of Ecology (Wald 1998) and to many alarmed congressional members such as Oregon senator Ron Wyden. In fact, as reflected in descriptions published in local and national newspapers, and as reflected in congressional and GAO reports, the Department of Energy sometimes appeared to even lack knowledge and interest in the Hanford problem.

It is not altogether clear why the Department of Energy seemed so slow to address the problems at Hanford. Being slow to act may have had something to do with the complex rules, agreements, and legislation DOE enforces and the kind of relationship that they had with the state, and with the contractors who were charged with the assessment and cleanup (General Accounting Office 1999; Senate 1995: 20–22). It may also have related to experts disagreeing about technical solutions (Murphy 2000b) or have reflected DOE's desire to avoid the negative publicity, local meetings, and congressional hearings that would surely accompany actions that publicly expose radioactive dangers (Geiger 1990; Murphy 2000a; Raloff 1990). DOE may have been slow because they simply did not want to know (Wald 1998), or it may have been related to the enormous costs of an effective cleanup, aptly described as "a river of money flowing out of Washington, D.C." (Schneider 1994: A-21; Senate 1995: 4–8). DOE's slowness may have been the result of really not understanding the extent of the problem, or more cynically, they may have wanted to keep a low profile on Hanford so they would reduce public opposition to their efforts to restart one of Hanford's reactors (Government Accountability Project 1999, 2001c).[3]

Problems simmered underground at Hanford, waiting to be addressed. Reporters continued to ask if the DOE was competent to be an environmental steward (Wald 1998). A crucial ingredient for getting the DOE's attention came from the grassroots activities of "the Downwinders," and organizations such as the Hanford Education Action League (D'Antonio 1993: chapter 4). But it would eventually take more than concerned-citizen groups, investigative reporters, worried workers, and attentive Congress members to move the Department of Energy to action. It would take whistleblowers.

Indeed, the Department of Energy was forced to seriously respond to the health and safety threats at Hanford starting in the late 1980s, because of the persistent actions of whistleblowers who began expressing alarm about the unchecked contamination at the site (D'Antonio 1993; Lynch 1999b; Murphy 2000a). Whistleblowers such as Casey Ruud, John Brodeur, and Jim Simpkin had the insider information, the public's attention, media coverage, and the ear of Congress. Their important role in moving the DOE toward action was captured in the headlines of an October 1999 issue of the *Seattle Times Magazine*. The headlines asked, "How Bad Were the Leaking Tanks? And Did Anyone but a Couple of Whistle-Blowers Really Want to Find Out?" (Lynch 1999b). Whistleblowers succeeded in directing attention and producing action to address the dangers of Hanford.

Of course, it would be "unfair" and "unwise" to rely on whistleblowers as the only "early alarm" warning of trouble or rely on them as *the* major anticorruption tool. Unfair because the personal cost to the individual whistleblower is usually so great; unwise because the uncovering of past misdeeds may misdirect agency attention away from the important ethical issues and choices of the day (Jos 1991). Ethicists agree that the best approach for organizations is to avoid misconduct in the first place. But if this hasn't happened, whistleblowers play a crucial role in cleaning up the mess.

However unfair and unwise, whistleblowers have been effective instruments for uncovering, exposing, and publicizing wrongdoing and serious health threats. But whistleblower Barbara Moulton did even more.

Barbara Moulton had a profound and lasting effect on the Food and Drug Administration in the early 1960s. In her case, whistleblowing did more than merely uncover problems and expose risks of harm to the public. Because of the particular circumstances, she was instrumental in averting a calamity and responsible for turning an agency's public exposure and embarrassment into a renewed commitment to their mission.

Barbara Moulton

Four decades ago, on February 19, 1960, a forty-four-year-old medical doctor named Barbara Moulton resigned her job at the U.S. Food and Drug Administration (FDA) and blew the whistle on the agency's questionable and corrupt practices in testimony to Congress. Hers was part of an "epidemic of resignations" (Senate 1960: 13104), but she chose not to resign in silence. She went public with her exposé and became a whistleblower before the term *whistleblower* was even coined.

Moulton's letter of resignation, addressed to the head of her agency, George P. Larrick, commissioner of the FDA, called for a "militant Food and Drug Administration," referring to "hundreds of people" who "suffer daily" and the many who die because "the Food and Drug Administration has failed utterly in its solemn task of enforcing those sections of the law dealing with the safety and misbranding of drugs, particularly prescription drugs" (p. 12021). The problem she addressed was the undue influence the pharmaceutical industry had over FDA decisions.

Moulton didn't send Commissioner Larrick her resignation letter; instead it was read into the *Congressional Record* and became part of the testimony that Moulton gave as a star witness in June 1960 before the Senate Subcommittee on Antitrust and Monopoly of the Committee on the Judiciary, chaired by Estes Kefauver (D-TN).

In two years, Moulton would see every one of her recommendations adopted by the FDA. The agency was transformed, but not solely because of her skills as a whistleblower and the merits of her arguments. Reform came because of the dramatic events related to the now notorious sedative Thalidomide.

Originally heralded as a "miracle" drug and a "wonder" drug (Grigg 1987), Thalidomide was "implicated in the birth . . . of thousands of armless, legless, earless, and otherwise malformed babies" (Lear 1962: 35). Moulton's whistleblowing, coupled with a great calamity, changed the FDA forever.

The Problem

In 1960, Moulton blew the whistle on what was described as a "cozy relationship" between the FDA and the drug industry. Years later, in an interview, she graphically described the inappropriately close ties between the drug industry and many of the people who worked at FDA. She said, for example, that in her work at FDA, while she "insisted on Dutch Treat, everyone else in FDA was wined and dined," by representatives of the drug industry (Moulton 1989).

The problem was "endemic," according to one of Moulton's colleagues, John Nestor (1989). The most flagrant and well-publicized example of the time was Henry Welch, who was chief of the Antibiotics

Division of FDA but also editor of two privately owned journals that were financially dependent on drug manufacturers. In fact, Welch purportedly earned a quarter of a million dollars in one year by using his position in FDA to organize drug symposia papers and to endorse drug industry–related products.

The publicized and well-documented example of Welch's conflict of interest concerned his involvement with a combination of antibiotics called Sigmamycin. *Saturday Review* called Welch the "chief blitzer" in an advertising campaign on behalf of the chemical ingredients in Sigmamycin, manufactured by Pfizer (Lear 1960: 37). In 1956, Moulton had been one of a number of scientists who criticized Welch for inflated claims that Sigmamycin brought the "blessings" of "synergistic combinations of drugs" and exemplified the "third era of antibiotic medicine."

Moulton was especially critical of the FDA's drug approval process for having standards that differed from division to division. For example, Welch's antibiotics division had a more lenient approval process than the new drug branch (p. 40). When she reviewed the evidence of safety and efficacy of Sigmamycin, whose praises as a "miracle" antibiotic Welch had sung, she found the tests to be below the expected standards for any new drugs, whether antibiotics or not.

The Whistleblower

Moulton tried to reform FDA from within. Seeking an in-house corrective of the situation, Moulton presented her supervisors with substantial data on the "tragic results from abuse of antibiotic therapy." She hoped to persuade them to strengthen the approval process and move it from Welch's division. But "the only answer she received was that Dr. Welch had a great reputation and added luster to the name of the Food and Drug Administration, and that nothing could or should be done against him" (Senate 1960: 12036).

Moulton was transferred against her wishes from the New Drug Branch even though she had just completed a month-long project where she showed why a particular drug application should not be approved. Moulton was transferred out because, she said, she "was not sufficiently polite to members of the pharmaceutical industry." At this time, the drug industry had so much influence over the agency that one of the large pharmaceutical firms had actually written the agency requesting that Moulton no longer be permitted to handle their new drug applications (p. 12037). This experience, she said, was a warning to others that "there is nothing but discouragement offered to those who advocate a more vigorous enforcement policy" (p. 12043).

Others testified to Moulton's influence and integrity. In an interview, Frances Kelsey, who was to become Moulton's successor, said that Moulton "was with the vanguard of reform" and that she had the "interest of the public and agency at heart" (1989). To her colleague, John Nestor, Moulton was a "heroine." When she blew the whistle in her congressional testimony, "she threw the first bomb" (1989). In addition, to Moulton's revealing testimony about the drug industry's influence over FDA, she was the first to suggest to the Kefauver Committee that in the drug area, one cannot "prove safety in a vacuum. . . . You must prove efficacy as well as toxicity" (Moulton 1989). Put simply, she was arguing that FDA should make sure that the drugs that are approved for sale perform to the standards promised, while causing no harm.

The status and talents of Senator Estes Kefauver helped whistleblower Moulton publicize her issues. Kefauver had become chair of the Antitrust and Monopoly Subcommittee in 1957 and two years later began an extensive and highly publicized investigation of prices in the drug industry (Nadel 1971: 112–128). He was adept at getting effective media coverage. He improved the chances for publicity and thus the chances for public education on the issue of FDA responsibility and drug safety.

But Moulton also attracted public attention, although at first she "did not get instant publicity from the hearings," she recalled. Nevertheless, her personal background helped draw attention to her whistleblowing and led to press coverage of many drug industry issues.

First of all, the noteworthiness of her family name set Moulton apart. She was a "member of a family long distinguished in American science (her father was founding director of the Brookings Institution, and her uncle was operating head of the American Association for the Advancement of Science [AAAS], and for a period only one other family name appeared more often than the Moulton name in *Who's Who in America*)" (Lear 1960: 41).

Her education, experience, and advanced training also gave her credibility with the press and public. She was a graduate of George Washington University Medical School; she had graduate training in bacteriology, holding an M.A. and passing preliminary exams for her Ph.D. She had advanced training in surgery, had taught anatomy at

George Washington University, and had also practiced medicine (Senate 1960: 12019).

In addition, that Moulton was a woman increased public interest in her in at least two ways. First, it was unusual, especially in 1960, for a woman to have her level of education and responsibility; that she was a "lady doctor" made hers a more interesting story. Second, consumers, those toward whom safety issues were geared, were considered to be mostly female, so that Moulton's gender may have given her more clout with women in raising issues of drug safety.

Finally, Moulton's whistleblowing had given her some notoriety as well. Her willingness to go public with in-house scandals and thereby lose her immediate livelihood called for great courage. The risks she took sparked interest in her issues. She was aware that reprisals would most certainly follow in her resignation and public testimony. Referring to those who shared her knowledge and her views but remained silent, she said,

> Few are willing to risk the security of their positions by stating those views publicly. They all have families to support, and I cannot blame them. I am fully aware that in making this statement I have jeopardized, perhaps irreparably, my own opportunities for future Government employment.
> Nevertheless, I feel so strongly the danger of a weak and ineffective regulatory program in this most vital area, that such a statement from one who knows the agency from the inside seems essential. (Nestor 1989)

Thus, her background, gender, and story combined to stir interest in her issues; with the Kefauver Committee, she had a platform to mount a fight for change.

Moulton's public testimony at the congressional hearings had an impact on the agency practices and procedures that she had tried unsuccessfully to change as an FDA employee. The specificity of her charges and the amount of detailed information she used to support her arguments to the committee added credibility. But while her exposure of the FDA resulted in important changes, according to Nestor, the FDA "was still not that scared of Kefauver" (1989).

The most dramatic part of the changes that followed Moulton's whistleblower hearings was a "forced resignation." Arthur H. Flemming, the secretary of Health, Education and Welfare (where FDA was then located), asked for Welch's resignation because of the publicity given to Welch's flagrant conflict of interest. Further investigations of Welch's activities continued. A second fallout from the FDA exposure was that Secretary Flemming called for two investigations into FDA's affairs; one investigation was scientific, the other, administrative. The scientific inquiry, carried out by a National Academy of Sciences panel, advised that Moulton's recommendation be implemented, that is, that laws be changed to require new drugs to be proved effective as well as safe. At this time, however, the FDA ignored the panel's advice.

The administrative investigation resulted in a report that addressed the close ties between industry and agency. The report urged an end to fraternization between FDA officers and drug makers. In January 1961, Commissioner Larrick's deputy circulated a memo to all FDA staff calling for obedience to the injunction against fraternization. It was an important first step. Although for some who worked in FDA, the change was seen as being on paper rather than in enforcement, as Nestor noted, "at least now, there were memos to quote" (1989).

Frances Kelsey

In addition to the important nonfraternization memo and the removal of Welch, Moulton's impact on the FDA was felt in the many ways that her forthrightness and clear ethical standards influenced her FDA successor, Frances Kelsey. This became clear almost as soon as Kelsey took office, for Kelsey had attended the Kefauver hearing to listen to Moulton's testimony. In fact, the two women became friends (Jonathan 1960: 43).

In September 1960, a few months after Kelsey started to work in FDA in the job vacated by Moulton, William S. Merrill Company submitted an application to FDA for permission to market a sedative called Thalidomide. Evaluating this drug application was Kelsey's first assignment. About that assignment she later wrote: "At that time, new drugs were cleared for marketing on the basis of safety claims alone. The agency had 60 days to reach a decision that safety data were adequate or to notify the sponsor of observed deficiencies in the application. Failure to communicate by the 60th day would result in automatic approval of the drug" (1988: 221).

From September 1960 until March 1962, when Merrill withdrew its application for the sale of Thalidomide in the United States, Kelsey studied the drug and resisted the continuous and direct drug company pressure to approve the drug. She also withstood drug company pressure placed on her through her branch chief, Ralph Smith.

Kelsey was even threatened on April 19, 1961, that a Merrill vice president would go to FDA commissioner Larrick to complain about her if she did not approve the drug soon (Lear 1962: 37). According to Nestor, who shared an office with Kelsey, the Merrill representative called her several times a day. In fact, after a while, Kelsey stopped answering her telephone.

Kelsey found too many puzzles connected to the drug that she thought must be solved before a thorough job of evaluating the drug could be done. No approval without a thorough evaluation was her firm stand. According to Kelsey, "Little was known as to how [the drug] was absorbed and distributed in the body. We thought this was of importance in this drug, since it behaved rather differently from other drugs which were rather closely related, and furthermore animal studies did not parallel human experiences" (Senate 1962b: 15). For example, it was a sleeping pill, yet it did not put animals to sleep and a person could not take an overdose of it.

While Kelsey continued her investigation and while she waited for the additional data on Thalidomide that she had requested from the drug company, she just happened to read in a British medical journal a short item that referred to a peripheral neuritis that seemed to accompany prolonged use of the drug. The item was only a letter to the editor from a doctor complaining of side effects of tingling, numbness, and coldness of the extremities that seemed to be caused by long use of Thalidomide and seemed to stop when the patient stopped taking the drug.

Kelsey was interested in the severity of the side effects, their frequency, and their reversibility; she asked Merrill for more data. On September 6 and 7, 1961, the drug company brought in a dozen investigators to argue that the side effects were minimal and reversible. Merrill continued to pressure for speedy approval.

Kelsey was strengthened in her resistance to drug company pressure by personal encouragement and support. The changed atmosphere in FDA (because of the new administrative rule) allowed her to be assisted by others. The deputy director of the medical division, Irwin Siegel, also resisted drug company pressure and acted as a buffer between Kelsey and both her branch supervisor and her division director. Siegel was "advising her every step of the way" and "kept her out of trouble," said co-worker Nestor (1989). Kelsey was also supported by other "Young Turks" in the FDA and by her pharmacologist husband who sat up nights with her trying to understand the chemical analysis that Merill had submitted with its application (Jonathan 1960: 43).

But most important, Kelsey was supported by Moulton, privately and because of public action. Moulton encouraged and privately "coached" Kelsey on "ways and means of avoiding some of the political booby traps Moulton herself had previously fallen into" (Kelsey 1989). Moulton's public impact was being felt. Her exposé of the FDA in the congressional hearings of the previous year had laid convincing groundwork for the accusation that the FDA had been captured by industry. Moulton's testimony helped pave the way for even bigger changes at the FDA. In fact, at this time, a case against Welch was about to go to a grand jury.

Thus Moulton had had a strong effect on Kelsey's actions in two ways. First, Moulton was a role model, mentor, and coach for how to maintain independence in evaluating a drug. Second, Moulton's independent and informed Senate testimony affected Kelsey's working milieu and thus contributed to Kelsey's ability to do her job effectively. Kelsey's insistence on taking the time that thoroughness required prevented a national tragedy.

The Calamity

On April 4, 1962, Helen Taussig, professor of pediatrics at Johns Hopkins University, left a phone message with former co-worker John Nestor. She had worked with him a decade before. Taussig had just gotten back from spending one month in Germany and two weeks in England and Scotland. She returned to the United States armed with statistics and photos demonstrating a link between Thalidomide and a serious birth defect called *phocomelia* (or sealed limbs).

Phocomelia was epidemic in Europe. Radioactivity, x-rays, contaminated food, and detergents were thought to be possible explanations for the condition; but in November 1961, a German doctor discovered a link with Thalidomide. This link was confirmed in Australia, then in Scotland.

Taussig came home concerned about protecting unborn children. Thalidomide had been distributed to more than three thousand women in the United States in the guise of a clinical test, but really as a part of a marketing promotion (Grigg 1987). Kelsey said, years later, that even she had not realized when she was evaluating the drug how widely it had already been disseminated. After Nestor spoke with Taussig, he connected her with Kelsey, so that Kelsey could hear the evidence.

By this time, because of the evidence from Europe, Merrill had withdrawn its application for approval from the FDA. Thalidomide was never allowed to be sold in the United States. Nevertheless, there were still thousands of U.S. citizens who were continuing to get the drug from doctors who had been disseminating it for "testing."

The all-too-cozy relationship between industry and agency meant that the FDA had not yet ordered withdrawal and had left it completely up to Merrill to contact the doctors to return or destroy the pills that were left. It was estimated that since 1959, a total of more than 2.5 million Thalidomide tablets had been distributed, as well as lesser quantities of liquids and powders containing the drug.

On hearing Taussig's report, both Kelsey and Siegel immediately wrote memos to Commissioner Larrick about the drug's connection with birth defects and emphasized the importance of stopping its use. No FDA action followed, for the commissioner did not feel that further action was part of FDA's responsibility. Taussig also wrote to Larrick and received only a curt note back. After two weeks of no FDA action, Nestor went to Larrick's office to find out why doctors had not been told to stop dispensing Thalidomide, given that the agency had the power to order and monitor the drug's withdrawal. No FDA action followed.

Months later, Commissioner Larrick still defended both his hands-off decision and Merrill's inadequate efforts to inform the medical profession although he knew at the time that some of the drug was still being used. Even the pressure of congressional hearings did not cause the FDA to take a more active role in withdrawing the drug from use. But public outcry did.

In May, Representative Emanuel Cellar (D-NY) had scheduled hearings for the House Antitrust Subcommittee. Taussig was called as a witness. On the projector that she brought, she displayed some gruesome pictures. The *Washington Post, Washington Star,* and *New York Times* all had representatives at the hearing. Nestor was among those who expected prominent media attention to be given to Taussig's message. But even though the press tables were filled, no articles saw print.

Nestor was so upset by the absence of publicity for this appearance that he called a Kefauver Committee staff member, E. Wayles Browne, to warn him that the aims of the upcoming Kefauver hearing were in jeopardy because of the lack of publicity on the issue. Nestor was alerting the staff member more than a month before the Kefauver Antitrust and Monopoly Subcommittee hearings were scheduled to begin in the Senate. His alerts prompted Kefauver to place a personal call to the editor of the *Washington Post* who had him talk to a young reporter, Morton Mintz, about the importance of the story and how it deserved press coverage. Mintz was assigned to cover the Kefauver hearings, which included, once again, Taussig showing her shocking slides.

In the belief that attention to Kelsey would make the *Washington Post* more likely to publish his stories, Mintz made her the focal point of his coverage. According to an FDA publication written twenty-five years later, it was Mintz's first article on July 15, 1962, that ignited the public. "This is the story of how the skepticism and stubbornness of a government physician prevented what could have been an appalling American tragedy," Mintz began. His story was picked up by the wire services and after that, according to William Grigg, then of the *Washington Star,* "You could not turn the pages of a newspaper, a news magazine, or picture magazine—nor even *Scientific American*—without these powerless, limbless infants staring up at you" (Grigg 1987). The public panicked over the issue of drug safety.

President John F. Kennedy had not supported strong consumer-oriented drug legislation. In early 1962, he had sent to the House and the Senate a weak bill developed without consulting Senator Kefauver (Nadel 1971: 25). But when the public learned about Thalidomide via national publicity, the drug's effects aroused "public horror," which was skillfully exploited by the senator (Quirk in Wilson 1980: 199; Meier 1985: 83). The Thalidomide crisis was likened to "the calvary coming to the rescue [of strong drug policy] at the nick of time" (Nadel 1971: 127).

By August 1, 1962, President Kennedy had changed his position. He was assuring the public that about two hundred FDA staff were working on the recall of the supplies of Thalidomide in this country and that he was urging Congress to tighten existing drug laws. That year, a landmark drug law passed with provisions that marked a major shift in drug policy: "The law tightened the safety requirements for testing new prescription drugs on human subjects and stipulated that patients be told if they are getting an experimental drug. The law required that drug companies report adverse effects during clinical tests and after marketing . . . , that a drug label carry the common or generic name of the product, as well as its commercial brand name; and that prescription drug advertising to doctors list side effects along with the benefits of the drug" (Grigg 1987: 17). Also included in the law was Barbara Moulton's recommendation that before approval a new drug must be proved effective as well as safe.

Tying It All Together

The change that Moulton had recommended in her Senate testimony was finally law. But in truth, important as the change of law was, this whistleblower's impact on these and related events went far beyond one new drug law. It is a rare whistleblower who has a chance to change so much. The issue, the timing, public sentiment, and political context were aligned and had much to do with her success.

Moulton had alerted Congress and the public to the dangers of close ties between the drug industry and the FDA. This public exposure helped change the climate and the rules within FDA and helped rid the agency of its biggest offender, Henry Welch. With her actions, Moulton became a model and mentor for Frances Kelsey, her successor in the FDA, who played the crucial role in the Thalidomide case. Moulton's whistleblowing in Congress and coaching in the agency made it possible for Kelsey to resist industry pressure. In this way, Moulton's actions helped avert a great tragedy and paved the way for the FDA to give more prominence in its policies to consumer safety.

Barbara Moulton acted before there were ample whistleblower protections that might have prevented agency retaliation and the loss of her job. Indeed, at the time she exposed wrongdoing in the Food and Drug Administration, in testimony in the U.S. Senate, the term *whistleblower* had not yet been coined to describe her behavior and was not in use in popular parlance. In the decades to follow, however, increasing protection of whistleblowers would be made available for an increasing number of employees. The next chapter describes these developments and these protections.

Notes

Portions of this chapter are drawn from Roberta Ann Johnson, "Barbara Moulton, Early Whistleblower," *San Jose Studies* (spring 1991) © San Jose State University Foundation, 1991.

1. This is the perspective of many organizations and agencies that are encouraging whistleblowing worldwide, as we will see in Chapter 6.

2. According to *New York Times* reporter Matthew L. Wald, in his 1998 article "Admitting Error at a Weapons Plant: Belatedly, Energy Department Deals with Leaks of Nuclear Waste," when engineers acted to reduce Hanford's radioactivity aboveground, their actions increased the problems underground. For example when "the soil at the surface had become contaminated" engineers "spread clean gravel on top to reduce the exposure of workers." But then they discovered that the gravel increased the flow of rainwater through the contaminated dirt. This resulted in the water "washing radioactivity toward the Columbia River even faster." Doing nothing would have been better. As it turned out, "without the gravel, surface dirt or plants might have absorbed the water and allowed it to evaporate, without percolating through the soil."

Furthermore, in his article "Radioactive Waste Seeps Toward Columbia River," Kim Murphy (2000b) of the *Los Angeles Times* reported about the disagreement over the DOE plan to get rid of the waste stored in tanks by separating the radioactive material from other toxic compounds. The plan called for the toxic compounds to be moved and treated at another waste repository and the nuclear waste to be injected into liquid glass and buried in the Nevada desert. Some scientists, however, disagreed with the solution, warning that the process of retrieval could result in spilling 1 million gallons of liquid, adding to the ground contamination.

3. The most cynical explanation for why DOE seemed unwilling to grapple with solving the problem and spending the money for a more effective cleanup had to do with their possible plans to restart the Fast Flux Facility Reactor (FFTF). In 1999, Secretary of Energy Bill Richardson asked the department to prepare an Environmental Impact Statement for restart of the Hanford reactor for what he said were civilian purposes—medical, research, and for the space program. However, the Government Accountability Project, which condemned the proposed restart of the reactor, charged that the real reason Secretary Richardson wanted to restart FFTF was to produce nuclear mini-weapons for use on the post–Cold War battlefield. Senator Ron Wyden also opposed the restart. He characterized a possible restart of a Hanford reactor as "one step closer to declaring nuclear war against the citizens of the Pacific Northwest" and was also quoted in GAP's press release of August 18, 1999.

GAP began a process to block the reactor's restart. They filed a "notice of intent to sue" over the "major conflicts of interest and extensive legal deficiencies" of the DOE's environmental study. GAP's press release of September 27, 2001, criticized DOE plans to privatize FFTF because they were planning to do so with the very company that prepared the environmental impact study. This was clearly, according to GAP, a conflict of interest.

5

Protecting the Whistleblower

R obert Jackson slipped into a San Diego pay phone, nervously dialed the downtown hotel where a congressman's aide was staying and whispered, "my life is in danger!"

Jackson was a whistleblower, a young sailor who reportedly had gathered "2,000 pages of Navy documents that showed case after case of fraud, forgery, and kickbacks aboard the aircraft carrier *Kitty Hawk*." He was arranging to turn over these materials to Congress "if in return Representative Jim Bates (D-CA) could keep him off the carrier's upcoming deployment and away from enlisted men who had threatened him" (Bunting 1985: 3).

This description of Robert Jackson's experience is a dramatic example of a fact of life for most whistleblowers, namely, that there are dire personal consequences for blowing the whistle. Reprisals are usually less severe than the bodily harm that Jackson feared, and are typically dismissal, transfer, demotion, and harassment.

The experience and impact of reprisals on the whistleblower has been a theme for many scholars and practitioners, from Ralph Nader in 1972, to Myron and Penina Glazer in 1989, and C. Fred Alford in 2001. What they and others have found is that in most cases of whistleblowing, instead of the problem raised by the whistleblower becoming the focus of attention, typically the individual whistleblower becomes the issue. The strategy has been referred to as "nuts and sluts," because, according to some whistleblowers, "their claims are ignored by finding them to be emotionally disturbed or morally suspect" (Alford 2001: 104).

"The government does not respond to the problems raised by

whistleblowers," says Louis Clark, executive director of the Government Accountability Project. "Instead the government makes the whistleblower the problem" (1978: 12). There is ample evidence to support this perspective. According to Frome (1978), "when a revelation is made public, the question inside the bureaucracy is not 'Is it right or wrong?' but 'Who leaked it?'" The attention is on the "squealer," the "damaged good" who is "ostracized" (Branch 1979; Weisband and Franck 1975) and who, according to Senator Howell Heflin, is often "sent to do-nothing jobs in undesirable locations, or [is] demoted or fired" (Senate 1983: 3).

The case of the sailor Robert Jackson amply illustrates this attitude. When he became a whistleblower, the navy imputed a range of "personal motives" to his action. Although he was portrayed as credible, having appeared on national television and in *Time*, *Newsweek*, and *People* magazines, the navy characterized him as a "bitter" and "vindictive" sailor, out "to get" the captain of the ship for not paying him enough for a training course he submitted through their suggestion program. Jackson, who was a "born-again Christian," was also portrayed by navy officials as an "evangelical troublemaker" (Bunting 1985: 10).

The list with names of whistleblowers who themselves became the issue abounds. Louis Clark (1978) describes the "favored ways" the bureaucracy reserves "to get" the whistleblower and points to nearly a dozen cases,[1] including that of the well-known whistleblower A. Ernest Fitzgerald.

A. Ernest Fitzgerald was an analyst for the Department of Defense who blew the whistle on cost overruns for the large C-5A cargo plane (Senate 1983: 150). Starting in 1965, he held the position of deputy for management systems in the office of the secretary of the air force.

The Lockheed Aircraft Corporation had contracted to design and build the C-5A. By 1968, they were seriously behind schedule and over budget and needed the federal government's C-5A contract to continue to be able to survive financially (Fitzgerald 1972: 212). Some members of Congress were opposed to additional funding for the plane. In October 1968, the Joint Economic Committee, chaired by Senator William Proxmire, held hearings on the subject, and Fitzgerald was invited to testify (p. 216).

Fitzgerald's superiors, knowing him as a critic of their procurement programs, "counseled" him to "stay away from the C-5A" in his testimony (p. 220). Unfortunately, Fitzgerald was specifically asked about the aircraft contract and he answered truthfully about the billions more than were estimated that it would cost (Westman 1991: 13).

Seven months later, Fitzgerald was again invited to testify in front of the Joint Economic Committee about another air force procurement. "I was strangely and uncharacteristically depressed by the array of power against me," he wrote (Fitzgerald 1972: 243). Although warned again not to be too forthcoming in his responses, once more he answered the legislators' questions truthfully and was critical of the project. By November 1969, Fitzgerald was notified that his agency position had been eliminated. It took ten years of creative litigation, including a lawsuit against President Richard Nixon, for Fitzgerald to be reinstated to his air force position (Westman 1991: 14).

What was demonstrated here, and is repeated in a wide and varied range of cases, is that the *whistleblowers* were consistently on trial, not the policies they had criticized and exposed. Fitzgerald complained, "We have turned the rewards and punishment system on its head. The people who make waves are discouraged, put down; their careers are destroyed, even if they win, as I have been said to have done" (Senate 1983: 150).

The pattern across countless examples, almost without exception, is that the individual whistleblower experiences reprisals. This is one of the major reasons why people do not blow the whistle (U.S. Merit Systems Protection Board 1993: ii; General Accounting Office 1992a: 2–4). Yet, even with this shadow of almost certain dire consequences, in the United States a legal tradition has helped to create an environment that encourages whistleblowing.

A National Tradition

Through the years, there has developed a growing legacy conducive to whistleblowing in the United States. However, it has not been universally supported. There are some lawyers, scholars, commentators, and administrators who remain troubled by public sentiment and legal practice and interpretation that they feel are overly sympathetic and encouraging of whistleblowing. For example, reacting to what she considered to be "efforts to enshrine" whistleblowing as an "absolute virtue," the late *Washington Post* writer Meg Greenfield warned that "we are letting a new enthusiasm get the better of memory and judgment" (1978: 112).

Armed with descriptions of cases, some critics fear, or may even have actually experienced, abuses of a system that supports whistleblowing (Diaz 1983: 157; Bunting 1985: 10; "High Cost of Whistling" 1977: 75, 77; Dirks and Gross 1974; Gilman 1989; Mason 1994). As one observer suggested, whistleblowers' "motives range from putrid to pure. While some are impelled by an acute sense of justice or public concern, others are like ants longing to be grasshoppers" (Ewing 1977: 88).

A few opponents of the whistleblower-friendly trend have argued that there is only a narrowly defined area in which whistleblowing is completely justified. It is when employees are themselves asked to do something illegal. This puts them in the position of choosing "between criminal liability and losing their jobs." When they refuse to break the law, they become whistleblowers. Only in such circumstances, these critics say, should whistleblowing employees be protected (Westman 1991: 2).

But many, perhaps most, whistleblower cases emerge from a gray area where the whistleblower employees are "not legally responsible" for the "suspected improprieties" and where some whistleblowers do not have "firsthand knowledge" or complete proof that their employers are guilty (Westman 1991: 2). While some may disagree on whether these whistleblowers, emerging from this "gray area," also deserve vigorous protection, U.S. law, nevertheless, protects them all.

Examining retaliatory discharge, Daniel P. Westman, documents the long-standing U.S. tradition of encouraging employees to report about wrongdoing and of protecting them when they do so. He refers to the 1863 False Claims Act, the development of labor law, and common-law protections in the interest of public policy, to make his point.

The False Claims Act

During the Civil War, Congress passed the False Claims Act to address the problem of profiteers who overcharged the government for scarce and needed wartime supplies. It was a serious public problem. Of these corrupt government contractors, President Abraham Lincoln said, "Worst than traitors in arms are the men who pretend loyalty to the flag, feast and fatten on the misfortunes of the Nation while patriotic blood is crimsoning the plains" (Helmer, Lugbill, and Neff 1999: 28). Congress was also concerned about this abuse. After lively debate in both houses (pp. 29–32), a supportive Congress passed the False Claims Act to address this problem.

The act relied on average citizens to uncover fraud; accordingly, it encouraged whistleblowing. By the terms of the False Claims Act, on behalf of the United States, private citizens could sue companies who were engaged in fraudulent activities (making false claims) with the government. The individual whistleblower actually became the plaintiff in False Claims Act cases. They were called or denominated the *qui tam* plaintiff, which means that they were suing in their own right as well as for the government.

When a citizen, the *relator*, decides to bring a *qui tam* action, they file a False Claims Act complaint in federal court under seal, providing the government with the necessary evidence. The Department of Justice (DoJ) has sixty days to investigate the claim and then to decide whether to join or to decline the lawsuit. Joining would contribute "muscle" to the claim because it means the government would assume lead responsibility for prosecuting. If the government declined to intervene, the citizen could always go ahead alone (Miethe 1999: 135).

The False Claims Act further encouraged *qui tam* lawsuits by rewarding them. It allowed citizens to recover a percentage of the amount the contractor overcharged. In 1986, protection for the whistleblower against retaliation was added to the False Claims Act. Between 1997 and 1999, almost 1,500 *qui tam* complaints were filed under the False Claims Act, and in 1999 alone, False Claims Act cases recovered a half billion dollars (Helmer, Lugbill, and Neff 1999: v).

Labor Law

Labor law was also a precursor to current whistleblower legislation. Over the past century, the development of labor law provided protections for employees and for the curbing of their employers' powers. The 1908 Clayton Antitrust Act, the 1926 Railway Labor Act, and the 1932 Norris–La Guardia Act as well as the Wagner Act (National Labor Relations Act) all established limits for employers' actions and areas of protection for employees.[2] By encouraging employees to oppose unfair labor practices, and by protecting them from retaliation, labor law laid a foundation for future antiretaliation measures (Westman 1991: 7).

Common Law Practice

In more than half the United States' judicial jurisdictions, courts have protected employees from being wrongfully fired in retaliation for their acting to further public policy. These are called common-law protections and there are three general circumstances that trigger them.

The first set of public policy circumstances that are used to protect employees from wrongful termination concerns employees who are discharged for refusing to commit an illegal act. The illegal violation they are asked to commit might be in highly vulnerable areas such as environmental law or medical care. But in some jurisdictions, the courts even protect employees from retaliation when they refuse to commit some private violation against an individual or when they refuse to act contrary to professional ethical standards. Under the public policy doctrine, employees are protected from wrongful discharge because they declined to perform the illegal act (Westman 1991: 84–91).

A memorable illustration of the public-policy doctrine was the 1985 Arizona case *Wagenseller v. Scottsdale Memorial Hospital.* An employee claimed to have been discharged because, in participating in a company skit, he refused to "moon" fellow employees. He was fired in retaliation and the court said he was wrongfully fired. They used the public policy doctrine to protect him; they said that the law he refused to violate was the law against indecent exposure.

In the second judicial area of protection, the courts have recognized the public policy doctrine in cases where employees are wrongfully discharged merely for exercising their rights. A common example, starting in the 1970s, has to do with workers' compensation. The courts have protected employees who allege they were wrongfully discharged in retaliation for filing for workers' compensation benefits. An employer who threatens discharge for this, they argued, clearly contravenes the public policy.

In this same category of protection, in over twenty jurisdictions, employees cannot be required to take a polygraph test as a condition of working. If they refuse and are discharged in retaliation, many courts have recognized their public policy cause of action and have protected them.

The third area of public policy doctrine protecting workers against retaliation is where an employee is discharged for carrying out an important civic duty (Westman 1991: 96–98). Examples of this occur when the courts protect employees who have been wrongfully discharged because of serving on a jury or serving as an election officer. The courts have reasoned that these are important civic duties and public policy is obstructed when employees are prevented from performing them.

In all these cases, and in all three areas of public policy doctrine (illegal acts, exercising rights, and civic duty), significant public health, safety, and well-being issues need to be implicated for the courts to intervene. But when the courts do intervene, they establish a principle that allows workers to be protected against unfair retaliation for something they have done.

Public Health and Safety

In the last decades, legislators have sought to protect against retaliation those who reported abuses in areas that were highly valued or safety-sensitive. On the federal level, the result was that whistleblower protection provisions were included in more than fifty federal statutes that regulate public health, well-being, and safety. These laws protect citizens from impure air and water, toxic waste dumps, unfair labor practices, dangerous workplaces, and civil-rights violations. The most comprehensive list available of these laws can be found in the appendix at the back of this book.

Employees in the private as well as the public sector are protected from retaliation if they expose violations of these acts. While there is a growing popular consensus that supports this protection effort, emerging from the private sector is the occasional practice of bribing whistleblowers into silence. In some private industries, companies actually pay whistleblowers to stop talking.

Because whistleblowing brings with it such high personal costs (loss of job, cost of lawyers, etc.) whistleblowers, once they begin to talk, will occasionally agree to accept money from their employers to keep silent. When this happens, the whistleblowers actually sign a contract, promising not to go public with their information in exchange for compensation, payment of outstanding legal fees, and an end to employer retaliation.

This was an especially troubling development because many of the "secret money for silence" settlements "muzzled" whistleblowers in the nuclear industry. The Nuclear Regulatory Commission at first respected these "contracts for silence" as legal, but then was forced to reverse itself in 1990, because of the pressure of imminent congressional public hearings. Now, in the nuclear field at least, the public is protected from these "money for silence" agreements.

However, "money for silence" contracts continued to be negotiated with other whistleblowers whose work areas fell under the Toxic Substance Act, the Occupational Safety and Health Act, Superfund, and laws regulating mine safety, clean air, and clean water. A confidential report on "Secret Money-for-Silence Agreements in the Nuclear Industry," compiled in May 1989 by the staff of the U.S. Senate's subcommittee on nuclear regulation, warned of the implications for safety of these arrangements (Aronson 1992).

Similar hush-money agreements were also negotiated in other areas such as equal employment cases and in False Claims Act proceedings. However, according to Stephen Kohn, all these "restrictive settlement provisions have not withstood judicial scrutiny." Through the 1990s, hush-money clauses in settlements have been made void by the U.S. Department of Labor, the Nuclear Regulatory Commission, and many courts (Kohn 2001: 369–370).

Whistleblower protections in seven of the health- and safety-related federal laws are explicitly enforced by the Department of Labor (DoL). Their procedures are time-sensitive. The whistleblower who believes he or she is a victim of retaliation has thirty days to file a complaint with the DoL, and DoL has thirty days to investigate and determine if the complaint has merit. If their decision is not acceptable to both parties, the case may then be heard by an administrative law judge. If the agency acted improperly, DoL can offer remedies of reinstatement, back pay, and compensatory damages to the whistleblower.

Department of Labor jurisdiction, however, does not guarantee a just outcome. A veteran manager in the California Pacific Gas and Electric (PG&E) utility company found that out.

From 1983 to 1998, Neil Aikens was a shift foreman for PG&E. For years, he complained publicly about safety problems at the Diablo Canyon nuclear power plant where he had worked. A major issue was the safety of new circuit breakers that did not fit easily with the old equipment.

PG&E's response to his safety complaints was to enlist the use of a psychiatric program they were required, by the Nuclear Regulatory Commission, to maintain. They sent Aikens for a psychological evaluation. He was assessed by the psychiatrists as having "paranoid delusions," and he was fired from his job. Aikens appealed. The DoL investigated the case because the nuclear-power law was one that fell within their jurisdiction. They uncovered a range of evidence that caused them to issue a report critical of the process and Aikens's diagnosis.

The suspicious evidence they found included the fact that one of the examining psychiatrists was specifically directed by PG&E executives on how to remove Aikens from office before he even interviewed Aikens. In addition, many of the other operators and managers who were interviewed believed Aikens to be mentally sound; other employees had complained about the same problem Aikens had complained about; and, in an unusual move, forty of Aikens's co-workers petitioned the Nuclear Regulatory Commission for him to be reinstated.

Armed with this range of evidence, the report issued by the Labor Department suggested that "the real problem was that Mr. Aikens had publicly embarrassed his superiors." PG&E reached a settlement with Aikens and he retired early. A settlement for Aikens could avoid uncertainty, publicity, and increasing legal bills. But a settlement also avoided a resolution of the case on its merits and thus it prevented Aikens from achieving some sort of official exoneration (Wald 2000: A-21).

State Protections

The state statutes protecting whistleblowers "address specific areas including health care, abuse of children and the elderly, foster homes, motor vehicle emissions, workers' compensation, and public utilities" (Vaughn 1999: 582). Laws in the fifty states are not uniform as to how and whether whistleblower protection is provided. States also vary as to whether they offer private- and/or public-sector whistleblowers protection from retaliation (Westman 1991: 62).

State protection also varies for whistleblowers who are state government employees. Thirty-five of the fifty states have adopted laws protecting them. With the exception of California, whose laws were passed in 1979, all the state protective legislation was passed during the 1980s. Whether state employees are encouraged to report wrongdoing, what agency they need to report to, whether they can be compensated for their difficulties and are protected from retaliation, and whether whistleblower identities are protected differ from state to state.

An "overwhelming majority" of state statutes protect disclosure by whistleblowers only when they go to "government officials and to public bodies" (Vaughn 1999: 597). A surprising number of state whistleblower statutes fail to address or to protect internal (within the agency) disclosures of whistleblowers (pp. 597–602). As to the motivation of the whistleblowers, most state statutes require that the whistleblowers "reasonably believe" the truth of their disclosure and some statutes specifically include a requirement for the whistleblower to "act in good faith" (p. 603). States also differ as to how well they guard against abuse by the whistleblowers themselves.

According to Robert G. Vaughn, in his analysis of state whistleblower statutes, the vast majority of them protect disclosures of violations of state law and a striking number of them include protecting disclosures of violations of federal laws. Three other frequently protected disclosure areas for state whistleblowers are government waste, substantial and specific dangers to public health or safety, and abuse of authority (pp. 588–592).

The fifteen states offering state employees no whistleblower protection may be providing them civil-service protections, but that is nowhere near as effective in protecting whistleblowers. Westman offers a summary of the relevant whistleblower statutes and coverage for all fifty states in his book on whistleblowing (1991: 52–60, 177–187).

We see a legacy being established. During the last century, an increasing number of employees began to be protected against wrongful retaliation and discharge. Courts started to protect employees in the name of public interest. And specific laws were passed on the federal level, and in most of the states, providing some whistleblower protection.

The Whistleblower Protection Act would represent a leap to a new level. Whistleblowers could now be protected, not because of the importance of what they did, or how they served the public interest, or connected to the environment or public safety. Now, nearly every federal employee who blew the whistle, no matter where they worked or what their issue, would be protected from retaliation and arbitrary discharge. Of course, it didn't happen that way all at once.

The Whistleblower Protection Act

The 1978 Whistleblower Protection Act, aimed at federal government employees, was so deficient in protecting whistleblowers against retaliation that its chief "protector," Special Counsel K. William O'Connor, publicly advised whistleblowers in 1984 that, "unless you're in a position to retire or are independently wealthy, don't do it. Don't put your head up, because it will get blown off" (Early 1984: A-19).

Under the terms of the act, a government whistleblower was required to go to the Office of Special Counsel, which would represent their case to the Merit Systems Protection Board (MSPB). But in ten years, of the approximately two thousand employees who used the process to protect themselves against retaliation, only four complaints of retaliation were upheld by the board. No surprise that the headlines for a whistleblower article in a newspaper for federal employees read, "Whistleblowers Need Protection—from their Protectors" (Devine 1988: 9).

Bertrand Berube, a whistleblower who was later vindicated and compensated, provided testimony to the system's gross inadequacy. "Through bitter experience," he said, "I can warn whistleblowers against entrusting their rights to the OSC." After Berube was fired by the General Service Administration (GSA), he went to the Office of Special Counsel for help. "It was a nightmare. OSC investigators grilled me under oath for five hours, but dismissed my complaint after 45 minutes of telephone calls to GSA," he said.

> The OSC wasn't satisfied just to rule against me. In congressional testimony the special counsel said I had engaged in "egregious insubordination," as well as a bureaucratic "shakedown" and "extortion." My crime? I had threatened to go public with my concerns about fire hazards, asbestos and other safety hazards at federal buildings, as well as about indefensible cost overruns, unless the agency stopped retaliating and started fixing the problems. (Berube 1988: A-22)

Joe Whitson's case, although in many ways quite different, also illustrates how unsympathetic the OSC was to the whistleblowers who sought its protection:

> Joe Whitson thought he was doing his duty when he testified at a 1984 court-martial on behalf of two sergeants accused of smoking marijuana. As chief of quality control at an Air Force drug-screening lab in Texas, Whitson pronounced his lab's procedures so sloppy that the evidence was useless. The charges were dropped. But when Whitson returned from the hearing, his superior told him he'd been reassigned with no duties to a basement office. Whitson turned to the Office of Special Counsel (OSC). . . . [Like others, he] didn't get much help. Three times he arranged, at OSC's request, for witnesses to meet with an OSC investigator; three times, Whitson said, the investigator failed to show. After struggling for two years to get his job back, Whitson finally quit the Air Force. (Noah 1989: 32)

As these examples demonstrate, although it was called the Whistleblower Protection Act, the procedures were flawed because they did not protect the whistleblower. In 1988, the process was revised. A new Whistleblower Protection Act passed unanimously in both houses of Congress. While President Ronald Reagan vetoed it, the next year Congress again passed it unanimously and it was signed into law by President George H. W. Bush.

The new version of the Whistleblower Protection Act went into effect on July 9, 1989. The Committee on Post Office and Civil Service provided oversight through its Subcommittee on the Civil Service. In addition to holding hearings, the subcommittee requested that the General Accounting Office "review the government's processing of whistleblower reprisal complaints and the Office of Special Counsel's effectiveness in protecting whistleblowers from reprisals" (General Accounting Office 1992a: 1).

The GAO reviewed a large number of employee cases of alleged reprisals for whistleblowing and compared the old and new whistleblower protection systems to see if there was a major difference in the number of cases and the way they were resolved. They randomly selected 406 of the 805 whistleblower cases that OSC had closed either for insufficient evidence or because they disproved the complaint. They wanted more information on the reasons OSC closed the cases.

They also gathered data on the disposition of 565 whistleblower complaints from employees who either appealed OSC's decision to the MSPB or went directly to MSPB with their whistleblower complaints. GAO only examined the outcomes, how the cases were disposed. It did not review for quality control, that is, for adequacy of investigation and appropriateness of OSC's and MSPB's dispositions of cases.

It appears, based on their report, that the provision in the revised act that had the biggest impact was the provision allowing employees to file appeals for themselves with MSPB, called an individual right of action. Employees using the new system no longer had to get a favorable decision from OSC to proceed.

Employees were able to file with MSPB if they did not like OSC's decision, if 120 days had lapsed without a decision rendered by OSC, or if they wanted to bypass OSC altogether. Of those who appealed directly to MSPB after not getting a satisfactory decision from OSC, fully one-third were getting relief, usually through settlements (sixty-seven of 213 complaints) and sometimes through reversals (eight of 213 complaints) (General Accounting Office 1992b: 4). Of those who bypassed OSC altogether, about one-third obtained relief from MSPB.[3]

The best and most thorough evaluation of the 1989 Whistleblower

Protection Act was the one that was painstakingly prepared by Thomas M. Devine and published in the *Administrative Law Review* in spring 1999. As a lawyer, and as someone who had worked with whistleblowers for decades as legal director of the nonprofit organization Government Accountability Project, Devine was sensitive to the difference between public pronouncements and actual protections.

The 1989 revised act provided a number of important changes: it (1) required new procedures for the Office of Special Counsel, (2) gave whistleblowers control of their own cases, (3) eliminated the need to prove the employer's retaliatory "motives," (4) reversed the burden to prove the connection between whistleblowing and retaliation, and (5) helped the whistleblower to get a job in a new agency, if they so chose.

The big disappointment in the revised law was that even with the shift to a lower burden of proof for the whistleblower, employees still found that proving reprisals was difficult. The good news was that the volume of complaints increased. The revised process was being used by many more people. The bad news was that the proportion of employees who could convince OSC that personnel action represented retaliation against them for exposing wrongdoing remained about the same.

"Under the 1989 Act, the principal reason for OSC's decisions to not pursue reprisal complaints" was the same one as the GAO reported in 1985—"the lack of sufficient evidence to establish a causal connection." In 1985, 64.5 percent of randomly selected complaints were closed by OSC because "it believed that the required causal connection could not be proven." After 1989, under the revised act, OSC cited this element in 55.6 percent of a randomly selected number of complaints (General Accounting Office 1992b: 5, 10, 13).

On March 31, 1993, citing how the OSC had not improved its success rate for securing relief for whistleblowers, despite the fact that the new law lowered the burden of proof for reprisals, Congressman Frank McCloskey, chair of the 1993 congressional oversight hearings on the Whistleblower Protection Act, issued a statement indicting the Office of Special Counsel. He said, "It is highly questionable whether federal whistleblowers are receiving adequate relief" from that office.

McCloskey described the fact that between July 1989 and September 1990, only *once* did OSC seek disciplinary action against employees who retaliated against whistleblowers even though OSC clearly has that power. In his statement, McCloskey specifically referred to criticism of OSC lodged by the Government Accountability Project. GAP, through their monitoring, had found much at OSC to criticize including the fact that OSC still did not "protect" whistleblowers and that OSC sometimes released information on whistleblowers' cases without the whistleblowers' consent (McCloskey 1993).

In GAP's formal testimony at the committee hearings, they called for the abolishing of the Office of Special Counsel, an office, they pointed out, that costs $8 million annually to run. Strategically, GAP studded their testimony with supporting evidence from a carefully analyzed survey they had done of a group of whistleblowers who had taken their cases to OSC. GAP used these cases to demonstrate that OSC was deficient in their evaluation of cases, conduct of investigations, and in their settlements (Devine and Ruch 1993: 2, 4–19).

GAP was also critical of the Merit Systems Protection Board, although they admitted the process had improved. They claimed that "on balance, an employee's chances of prevailing under the whistleblower defense at the MSPB ha[d] improved from the odds of winning the lottery to losing at Russian Roulette . . . better, but . . . not good enough" (Devine and Ruch 1993: 3). GAP noted that the percentage of whistleblowers whose cases prevailed on their merits at MSPB, after the revised act became effective, was dropping; the success rate dropped during the second year of the revised bill to only one-third of the first year's rate. Much of GAP's criticisms and recommendations for improving MSPB had to do with legal interpretation, practices, and procedures, all of which could be "fixed" by a Congress that can make its legislative intent clear.

On October 8, 1994, Congress acted to strengthen the Whistleblower Protection Act. The amendments they passed plugged holes, improved procedures, and provided additional safeguards for whistleblowers.

The 1989 law was improved in at least twenty areas. Among them were changes that made labor-management arbitration fairer to the whistleblower, and provisions that assured whistleblowers would receive damages (attorney's costs, settlements, etc.) if they won. The amendments also created punitive consequences for managers held responsible in agencies guilty of retaliation, outlawed general discrimination against the whistleblower instead of a more narrow list of prohibited action, prohibited OSC's abuses of discretion, especially leaks of information, and specifically rejected and overturned fourteen MSPB and federal circuit court decisions as illegal. Also significant was that the amendments stopped the management practice of retaliating by ordering the whistleblower to take "psychiatric" fitness-for-duty examinations (Devine 1999: 565–572).

Other changes affected how well the 1994 amendments were implemented. Starting in 1996, new personnel at the Merit Systems Protection Board, and in 1998 a new special counsel at OSC, helped establish new whistleblower protections (Devine 1999: 573–576). Many cases could illustrate the effectiveness of the Whistleblower Protection Act, as amended. The 2000 example of Neil Jacobs is one such case.

The Neil Jacobs Story

Neil Jacobs served as assistant district director for investigations in the Dallas regional office of the Immigration and Naturalization Service (INS) and had been working for the agency for twenty-seven years. Through the years, he had gotten high performance reviews and had been honored for the quality of his work. He was recognized at the White House with an award for supervising a program that replaced illegal aliens with former welfare recipients who were legal workers. His work was also recognized by the Ford Foundation with an Innovations in American Government Award.

In October 1998, Jacobs was a witness in Congress for the Subcommittee on National Security, International Affairs, and Criminal Justice of the House Committee on Government Reform and Oversight. In his congressional testimony, Jacobs exposed abuses including possible fraud involving the Dallas office's processing of 10,000 naturalization applications. He alleged that they bestowed U.S. citizenship without the necessary background checks and that many applicants were ineligible, some with felonious convictions. The Dallas regional office evaluated his job performance, suspended him for twenty-one days, and reassigned him to a nonsupervisory position.

Jacobs claimed the suspension and reassignment was in retaliation for his testimony. After an investigation, the U.S. Office of Special Counsel agreed. They represented him and succeeded in getting an indefinite stay of his reassignment. In May 1999, the OSC requested that the INS provide corrective action to Jacobs and when the INS failed to respond, OSC petitioned for corrective action and the case went to a hearing in front of an administrative law judge.

A settlement was reached and in March 2000, the MSPB chief

administrative law judge approved it. By its terms, Jacobs would receive a reassignment to the Hawaii district office in a position of equal grade and pay to his own; relocation expenses would be paid and his annual leave and hours of sick leave would be restored. Further, his attorney fees and back pay with interest and retirement contributions for his suspended days would be reimbursed (Office of Special Counsel 2000).

It did take well over a year's time to address and remedy the retaliation Neil Jacobs experienced because of his whistleblowing. But the Whistleblower Protection Act did work; after an investigation, OSC became his advocate and produced an attractive settlement for him.

More recently, unfavorable rulings from the federal circuit court have weakened whistleblower protections, and by 2002 support in Congress was growing for new amendments to overturn the court decisions. The new legislation (S. 995 and H.R. 2588) also included provisions to "close the security clearance loophole" so that national-security whistleblowers, who since 1985 were exempt from the protections of the law, would be protected (Government Accountability Project 2002a: 7).

Hotlines

Hotlines to report waste, fraud, and abuse were established in Inspectors General offices in federal agencies with the passage of the Inspectors General Act of 1978. While they have stimulated tremendous use, they also have received mixed reviews for fairness and effectiveness.

In November 1989, the GAO assessed the operations of twenty-five of these federal fraud lines as to accessibility, advertising, and staffing. Their judgment was that they were operating well. Twenty-two of the twenty-four had round-the-clock accessibility; the hotline staff received periodic formal training; and the hotline advertising was generally aimed at "appropriate" audiences. But the GAO, as well as other groups, also criticized the hotlines and the way they worked.

Hotline Critics

In their 1989 evaluation of federal government hotlines, the GAO pointed to some deficiencies. They suggested that the location of the hotline telephone number listings could have been improved. In addition, they pointed out that some agencies did not have toll-free lines (General Accounting Office 1989). But these observations were mild compared to other critiques.

The 1989 study of these agency hotlines by the American Federation of Government Employees (AFGE) was much more critical. The AFGE expressed grave concern about the confidentiality of hotline reports and the protection of whistleblowers. They also reported the results of a hotline survey in which 593 federal AFGE members responded to an AFGE questionnaire covering all federal agencies.

In the AFGE survey, nearly half of the respondents were unaware of the agency hotline; 87 percent didn't know the hotline telephone number, 62 percent didn't know where to get the number, and only 22 percent had seen the hotline number posted in their work area. When the respondents were asked to whom they would report an abuse, 31 percent said the fraud hotline, but almost as many, 29 percent, said their union. When asked why they did not choose the hotline, nearly half feared retribution or compromise of confidentiality; 27 percent did not think it would do any good (Sturdivant 1989).

The Project on Military Procurement, a group that has been working with military whistleblowers since 1981, also expressed a very critical perspective on federal hotlines to the GAO in 1989, and in testimony at Senate hearings. They characterized hotlines as luring "unsuspecting sources towards potential professional suicide."

The Project on Military Procurement pointed to two very serious problems relating to hotline investigations. First, once whistleblowers report wrongdoing, they are shut out of the process of investigation. This is especially unfortunate because often it is only the whistleblower who can lead investigators to the inside information to validate their claim.

A second problem described by the Project on Military Procurement is the tendency of the bureaucracy to kick the information down to the responsible level of management. Although they are the ones who oversee the activity in question, it often turns out to be the whistleblower's boss who is responsible for the fraud. Not only does this give the wrongdoer time to cover his or her tracks, but the information sent down can pinpoint the original source of the information, that is, the whistleblower.

The Project on Military Procurement testified that whistleblowers did not have confidence in either the effectiveness of the hotlines or its promise of anonymity (Rasor 1989). These weaknesses were illustrated by the inadequate hotline investigation in the Nancy Kusen case, described in Chapter 1. Nonetheless, federal hotlines consistently receive an enormous number of calls, and government departments claim they have been an unqualified success.

Hotline Supporters

Many federal agencies have boasted about their hotline's lure and success. For example, the U.S. Department of Labor has advertised its hotline number with a picture of a telephone and the catchy phrase, "You've Got Our Number: Call." Based on the Department of Labor's own account, whistleblowing within the department during the late 1980s resulted in their Office of Inspector General's (OIG) auditors questioning the expenditure of over $1 billion, over half of which was determined to have been improperly spent. During this same period, almost 4,700 criminal indictments and 3,600 convictions resulted from the OIG investigations (Hyland 1989: 1).

In 1989, the Department of Defense hotline alone received one thousand calls per month (Whitlock 1989) and calls and letters to the DoD hotline from October 1988 to March 1989, according to the department, resulted in 1,786 substantive allegations (Department of Defense Inspector General 1988–1989: vi). There is even a clause included in DoD contracts that requires all contractors bearing contracts for over $5 million to display the DoD hotline poster or have a comparable hotline program (Whitlock 1989).

Over a decade ago, the then secretary of defense, Dick Cheney, personally requested that the DoD hotline be publicized throughout the agency to "emphasize" President Bush's and his (Cheney's) "personal commitment to the reduction of fraud, waste, and mismanagement in Defense Programs" (Cheney 1989).

Throughout the 1990s, the volume of fraud, waste, and mismanagement complaints in DoD received through telephone calls and letters continued to be high. "In fiscal year 1991, the hotline received 9,270 telephone calls and 1,730 letters, totaling 11,000 contacts. In fiscal year 1992, 12,268 telephone calls and 1,938 letters were received, totaling 14,206 contacts—a 23 percent increase over 1991" (Department of Defense Inspector General 1992: 4-1, 4-2). In 1997, during a six-month period (April to September), the DoD hotline received 8,220 calls (Department of Defense Inspector General 1997: 30).

Whistleblower Hotline Posters by the U.S. Dept. of Defense,
the U.S. Dept. of Labor, and the U.S. Dept. of Commerce.

Congress mandates that the agencies record what happens to these calls and these callers. For example, every six months DoD does its own assessment on how well the hotline is working. All departments are required to prepare semiannual reports to Congress on how they are curbing fraud and waste and how they are improving department management. The DoD report includes a section on their hotline.

In March 1993, the DoD claimed that, since its inception, the hotline had saved the department over $163 million. "These savings were achieved as a direct result of investigations, inquiries, or audits launched in response to information provided by military personnel, Government civilians and private citizens" (Department of Defense Inspector General 1993: 4-1, 4-2). The department analysis claimed that one-third to one-half of those contacting the DoD hotline were making substantive charges and one-sixth to one-quarter of all the calls triggered "action"—an investigation, an audit, or an inspection (Department of Defense Inspector General 1992; 1993: 4-3).

For example, in the hotline section of their semiannual reports, the Defense Department, in 1992 and 1993, reported "significant investigative findings originating from hotline contacts" in categories such as funding irregularity, false or fraudulent claims, and cost overruns and contract overcharging. In each of two reports (September 1992 and March 1993) they listed at least one multimillion-dollar settlement resulting from a hotline contact. By 1997, the Defense Department claimed a cumulative department savings of $391 million as a result of hotline information (Department of Defense Inspector General 1997: 30).

The National Performance Review

The most well known hotline thus far has been the National Performance Review hotline, created in 1993 during the first month of the Clinton administration. Although there was some mention of ferreting out fraud, waste, and abuse, the major goal of the hotline was to achieve efficiency, "customer" satisfaction, and bureaucratic streamlining.

The Performance Review was the most publicized national hotline ever established and it was patterned after a Texas program started two years earlier. A team of 100 auditors, from sixteen Texas state agencies, interviewed hundreds of state employees and fielded thousands of citizen calls. At the end of five months, the Texas Performance Review presented recommendations for a $4.2 billion savings. The Texas legislature adopted over 60 percent of the recommendations totaling a savings for the state of $2.4 billion. A second similarly organized Texas review, in 1992, resulted in recommendations on ways to save another $4.5 billion (Gore 1993a).

The Clinton initiative also experienced a vigorous public response. In March 1993, as part of his "streamlining government" effort, the DoD hotline number and several other departments' hotline numbers were published in newspapers across the country with articles soliciting recommendations for improvement and reports of waste and inefficiency. During a three-week period after the hotline numbers were advertised this way, the DoD hotline alone received 4,061 calls.

Tying It All Together

Chief Justice Earl Warren once said that "law floats in a sea of ethics" (Cooper 1979: 78); for over one hundred years, many laws and practices protecting whistleblowers have been floating in the United States' ethical ocean. The False Claims Act, passed during the Civil War and resurrected with great fervor during the last few decades, twentieth-century federal labor law, and the many court common-law interpretations of "public policy" across various states all offered some protection to some of the employees who came forward to report and expose wrongdoing.

In addition, starting in the 1970s, Congress passed a number of federal laws that included special whistleblower-protection provisions. In these laws there were sections that prohibited "adverse actions by employers against employees who assist in carrying out the regulatory purpose of the legislation" (Chalk and von Hippel 1979: 51). Many of these laws were in the environmental field such as the Federal Water Pollution Control Act Amendments of 1972, the Toxic Substances Control Act of 1976, and the Clean Air Act Amendments of 1977. In the next decades, dozens more federal statutes and some state statutes followed in providing such protections.

For its sheer impact, however, the most significant protective statute was the Whistleblower Protection Act, passed in 1978 and amended in 1989 and 1994. This legislation aimed to protect all federal government employees, no matter what laws they were implementing and where they worked. Over half the states and some local governments have enacted similar legislation protecting state workers.

The federal Whistleblower Protection Act had a disappointing start. For years, the act promised more than it delivered because the Office of Special Counsel did not seem to champion the whistleblowers who sought its help. But in its 1989 revised form, the act allowed employees to circumvent the Office of Special Counsel and take their retaliation claim directly to the Merit Systems Protection Board. Although the Merit Systems Protection Board has its critics, at least at MSPB, approximately one out of three whistleblower claimants were getting some kind of settlement. Congress acted to revise the law in 1994, and is considering revising it again in 2002. With the 1994 congressional changes in the MSPB, procedures improved in at least twenty areas and better safeguards and new personnel are helping strengthen whistleblower protection.

The establishment of federal agency hotlines, in 1978, also represented a significant contribution to whistleblowers. Critics have argued that the federal hotlines are not well-enough known and are far from user-friendly, but agencies boast large numbers of contacts and large monetary savings because of them. There are data that can be used to support both positions. No studies, as yet, have analyzed, unraveled, and evaluated the way politics, merit, and luck determine how hotline cases are handled.

Whistleblowers represent a mixed bag of characters. There are devils and angels in the group; not every whistleblower seeks revenge and not every well-intentioned whistleblower is amply rewarded and protected. Take the case of Robert Mallozzi.

Robert Mallozzi

Twenty-six-year-old Robert Mallozzi had been an investigator at the Connecticut State Labor Department for a year when he blew the whistle on cheating on unemployment benefits. Realizing that the system needed tightening up to protect itself from cheaters, Mallozzi applied for unemployment with deliberate errors and false claims and watched as his application sailed through his agency.

To protect himself before he prepared the false application, he let others know of his plan and he signed an affidavit with two former co-workers. He also sent registered letters to Governor Ella Grasso and the state commissioner of labor, Frank Santaguida, describing what he had done. In response, he received a form letter from the governor's office thanking him for his interest and from the Labor Department he received a warrant for his arrest.

Perhaps Mallozzi's whistlebower plan was a little too creative. His case went to trial, where he won exoneration. Defending himself cost him expensive legal fees and personal trauma. Even with a not-guilty verdict, he realized that "if it doesn't go beyond that in tightening up the system," it was "a waste." And even after he had won his case, the department did not respond by employing the safeguards that Mallozzi detailed in his letters (*Newsweek* 1977: 75).

The United States' record is not perfect in supporting and protecting its whistleblowers, even the ones with the best of intentions. But that does not stop the United States from exporting the whistleblowing idea and encouraging it abroad. Chapter 6 will examine that theme.

Notes

1. Louis Clark, in "The Sound of Professional Suicide" (1978), also lists Dr. J. Anthony Morris, a urologist in the FDA, who blew the whistle over questionable practices of the swine flu immunization program; Stanley Mazaleski, a scientist with the National Institute for Occupational Safety and Health, who blew the whistle to get tighter controls over chloroform and cadmium; and Arthur Palman, a personnel specialist in one of the regional offices of the General Services Administration, who blew the whistle on the operation in his office of a "spoils system."

Ted Gest, in a 1981 *U.S. News & World Report* article, lists other examples, including the cases of William Deford, an engineer with the Tennessee Valley Authority who was concerned with safety problems in their nuclear power plants; Edward Rohrmann of the U.S. State Department, who worked in the New York Passport Office and blew the whistle on fellow workers issuing illegal passports; Bertrand Berube, an official in the GSA who tried to expose wasteful spending "to the tune of $1.5 billion"; and Joseph Pitchford, foreman of the federal prison in Ashland, Kentucky, who tried to expose procurement irregularities by blowing the whistle.

2. The Clayton Antitrust Act of 1914 specifically exempted labor unions that peacefully picketed from antitrust restraints, thus limiting the power of the employers. Employers, however, still had the right to fire whomever they wanted-ed. In 1926, the Railway Labor Act protected employees of the railroad from being coerced by their employers to join or not join a union. In 1932, the Norris–LaGuardia Act reaffirmed that employers could not use an injunction to stop employees from organizing. The Wagner Act, known as the National Labor Relations Act, nationally established the principle of collective bargaining that limited an employers' right to fire employees and included antiretaliation provisions. Daniel P. Westman, in *Whistleblowing: The Law of Retaliatory*

Discharge (1991), uses these examples to illustrate the theme that labor laws were the precursors of whistleblower protection.

   3. "According to an MSPB official," as quoted in the General Accounting Office report (1992b), starting on page 14, "there are two primary reasons for the high percentages of settlements and reversals. First, the official said that the MSPB trains its employees on finding alternative ways of informally resolving disputes, and MSPB emphasizes settling disputes rather than determining who is right. Second, he said that MSPB is the final place to resolve disputes, unless one of the parties chooses to pursue the case in the United States Court of Appeals for the Federal Circuit. Therefore, both parties may be more willing to come to a resolution rather than pursue the dispute any further."

6

Whistleblowing as an Export

B y the 1990s, whistleblowing had become more common, more accepted, and more protected. Like so much else that is "American," this seemed bound to have influence beyond U.S. borders. The United States began to export whistleblowing.

U.S. groups such as the Government Accountability Project offered technical assistance on whistleblower protection, and shared whistleblowing techniques with other developed democracies, including Canada, England, Israel, and Australia.[1] But the majority of the effort was focused on a different set of countries. Whistleblower advocacy emerged, embedded in an ambitious global reach. It was part of a larger U.S. mission to address corruption and improve democracy in developing countries and in the newly independent states of the former Soviet Union.

A wider world context—international organizations, international agreements, and an interconnectedness—also buoyed U.S. efforts. International organizations such as the World Bank and Transparency International helped with funding and training. The globalization of economies and technology made the sharing of whistleblower information and ideas easier. And formal international agreements such as the Organization for Economic Cooperation and Development and the Organization of American States' Inter-American Convention Against Corruption increased receptivity.

The reasons given for encouraging and protecting whistleblowers were mixed—to protect freedom of speech, encourage democracy, increase citizen responsibility, and address problems of corruption.

U.S. practitioners, advocates, ethicists, and academics were part of the process. They wrote and taught about good government practices and democratic values. Whistleblower protection was included in their prodemocracy packages and anticorruption programs. Well-attended international conferences were an effective venue for sharing ideas and programs.

International Conferences

International conferences widened and strengthened the connection between people and nations. They made networking faster and easier. International conferences also helped give whistleblowing advocates a worldwide arena.

As countries grew more interconnected in a global economy, economists warned that the presence of corruption could seriously impede a country's development (Mauro 2000; Abramov 2001). Corruption could reduce foreign investors, consumers, and moneylenders. Increasingly, there were more international conferences focusing on "ethics" and on "corruption" and they offered a venue that stimulated both the exchange of ideas and technical assistance. Many government officials and members of the business community attending these meetings were encouraged to include whistleblowing and whistleblower protection as part of a remedy for corruption.

Often these conferences were regional, such as the Organization of American States conference held in Guatemala or the many Newly Independent States conferences and workshops held in places like Slovakia, Georgia, Albania, Romania, and Ukraine. But some conferences advertised widely and aimed for a big international attendance. At virtually all these conferences, the subject of individual responsibility was highlighted.

Among the many examples of international anticorruption conferences held during the 1990s that attracted large numbers of participants were the "Ethics in the Public Service" conferences, with annual meetings at locations varying from Stockholm, Sweden, to Brisbane, Australia; international conferences in Jerusalem, Israel, on "Ethics in the Public Service"; and the semiannual "International Anticorruption" conferences sponsored by Transparency International and held at sites such as Durban, South Africa, and Prague, Czechoslovakia.[2]

International conferences attracted a wide range of attendees.

Government officials and multinational businesspeople from around the world, as well as representatives of international agencies such as the United Nations, were present at many of these meetings. For example, the director of the U.S. Office of Government Ethics regularly attended the annual conference of "Ethics in the Public Service." As a participant, he enthusiastically disseminated information about his office, provided lists of available published documents, and produced materials for other conference participants.

Toward the end of the 1990s, whistleblower protection was definitely part of the ethics training the United States endorsed. The Clinton administration sent a positive signal about whistleblowing to the rest of the world when, in February 1999, the United States hosted an anticorruption conference, "The Global Forum Against Corruption," initiated by Vice President Al Gore.

Government representatives from a hundred countries accounted for a conference attendance list of over 1,500. The conference's "guiding principles" included whistleblower protection as part of its list of identified effective anticorruption practices (Leventhal 2001).

Whistleblower protection was becoming an important part of the U.S. government agenda.

GAP and the State Department

For decades, the Government Accountability Project, a nonprofit organization based in Washington, D.C., had raised consciousness and helped pass and change laws concerning whistleblowers' rights in the United States. Because of the group's reputation, their anticorruption efforts, and their work on whistleblower protection legislation, GAP was tapped by the U.S. State Department, starting in the late 1990s, to engage in a kind of international "outreach."

GAP's years of experience and their many successes with U.S. whistleblowing issues (as described in Chapters 1 and 5) made them a perfect candidate to host foreign representatives visiting the United States who were interested in legal and practical issues related to whistleblowing. And there were many visitors.

In less than a four-year period, from 1998 to 2001, representatives from nongovernmental organizations (NGOs) from nearly fifty different countries visited GAP's District of Columbia office for advice, information, counseling, support, and inspiration.[3] According to Tom Devine, GAP's legal director, fully 95 percent of these visitors had been sent there by the State Department (Devine 2001c).

GAP also was invited to visit other nations to render technical assistance. GAP was asked to develop, evaluate, or improve their whistleblower protections and assist in their domestic anticorruption campaigns. These trips were usually arranged by foreign NGOs but the trips themselves were often paid for by the U.S. State Department.

GAP's first foreign visit was to Great Britain. Public Concern at Work, a nonprofit organization, asked them to testify, in 1998, on behalf of British whistleblower protection legislation, the Public Interest Disclosure Act.[4] GAP helped the organization mount a successful campaign resulting in the act's passage. Many GAP trips to Great Britain followed.

In a relationship that started in early 1999, GAP began collaborating with a Russian NGO called Siberian Scientists for Global Responsibility. GAP sponsored conferences, rendered technical assistance to Russian citizen groups, and made many on-site visits to Russian nuclear weapons facilities to work with Russian activists and NGOs. GAP built on their own experience and success with U.S. nuclear whistleblowers (Devine 1997: 5–7).

During their visit to Tomsk-7, the world's largest nuclear complex, GAP's water and soil nuclear pollution tests revealed contamination problems much bigger than Hanford's (see Chapter 4). GAP strategized with their Russian hosts about how to best expose the information to the public and to authorities. GAP was there, in part, to teach the Russian NGOs how to whistleblow (Government Accountability Project 2001a).

The U.S. Embassy in Bratislava, supported by the American Bar Association and Transparency International, sponsored a regional anticorruption conference in Slovakia in June 2001. The U.S. State Department sponsored GAP's participation.

GAP's keynote address on free speech and whistleblowing spurred so much interest by the region's NGOs and government representatives that they asked if Tom Devine, the GAP presenter, could return for a follow-up presentation on whistleblower protection. He returned for a two-day roundtable in October 2001, where he began to work with them on getting a free-speech bill passed.

There were many other trips. For example, after collecting 100,000 signatures on a petition on behalf of whistleblower rights, a South Korean NGO invited GAP to visit and assist them in preparing whistleblower legislation. The visit represented an important beginning although the Korean legislative efforts failed and the reform bill did not pass.

Australian meat inspectors invited GAP to help them deal with the problem of contaminated food, a problem exposed by Australian whistleblowers and an issue that could potentially affect U.S. consumers because of trade arrangements. While there, GAP worked with members of the Australian parliament and Australian NGOs on whistleblower protection issues.

Canada also called on GAP for technical assistance. FAIR, a Canadian NGO, invited GAP to help them pass whistleblower protection legislation. In the process, GAP developed an anticorruption model law that they continued to use for their work in other countries. In fact, the model law they developed in Canada was the basis for GAP's work with the Organization of American States (OAS).

Invited to Guatemala to participate with the OAS's working group on Probity and Public Ethics in March 2000, GAP went on to develop a checklist for effective whistleblower protection laws. It became a generic model for developing whistleblower protection legislation. Most OAS member countries had ratified the Inter-American Convention Against Corruption and one of its key corruption-prevention measures was whistleblower rights. The working group approved the model whistleblower law, an important first step toward the article's actual implementation.

The State Department also arranged a GAP trip to Mexico in fall 2000. GAP was invited to meet with municipal, university, and NGO representatives to talk about whistleblower rights and Mexico's anticorruption campaign.

The United States Agency for International Development

The U.S. government was encouraging whistleblowing abroad through other programs. The United States Agency for International Development (USAID), a forty-two-year-old federal agency that provides foreign assistance and humanitarian aid, was involved in such projects.

As part of its anticorruption efforts, USAID produced and widely disseminated *A Handbook on Fighting Corruption* (USAID 2001b).

Individual accountability and whistleblower protection were a prominent part of the USAID *Handbook*'s list of "recommended institutional reforms" (Leventhal 2001). In its sections on "Hot-lines and Whistleblower Protection," the *Handbook* describes how hotlines improve accountability but warns about the risk of retaliation. For that reason, USAID recommended to other countries that they provide whistleblower protection and in some cases reward whistleblowers as an anticorruption measure (USAID 2001b). USAID even helped set up a hotline in Bulgaria with the help of the international organization, Transparency International (USAID 2001b).

In addition, USAID sponsored Citizen's Advocacy Offices (CAOs) to further encourage whistleblowing. A CAO "serves as an active source of legal support for citizens and businesses with grievances concerning corrupt officials." It operates independently of government and provides free legal advice, representation in court, and helps citizens "gather and submit evidence in cases of alleged corruption" (Transparency International 2000).

In July 1999, USAID established two CAO offices in Donetsk, Ukraine, each with a twenty-four-hour telephone hotline. They were widely used. The CAO also served as a model and was designed to be part of a larger strategy for local NGOs to follow. The CAOs had a significant impact, as the following, just one of many stories, illustrates.

Among the whistleblowers the Donetsk CAO assisted was the captain of a cargo ship who exposed the wrongdoing of administration officials who were embezzling funds. In retaliation, the captain was "wrongly accused" and sentenced to prison. The CAO assisted the captain in getting his conviction set aside and his sentence "quashed." The CAO then prepared claims against the accused officials (Transparency International 2000).

The Organization for Economic Cooperation and Development

Another important U.S. government stimulus for change was the creation of the Organization for Economic Cooperation and Development (OECD). The seeds for OECD originated with the statutory prohibition against U.S. businesses using bribes to get business contracts, including contracts negotiated in other countries.

In the summer of 1997, with State Department encouragement, thirty-three of the world's wealthier nations, which were focused on better-ing the climate among major exporting countries, agreed to a "no bribery" principle. This "convention on combating bribery of foreign public officials in international business transactions" committed the countries to extending the "no bribery" rule to all exporting countries. It was signed in December 1997 and "entered into force" on February 15, 1999 (Department of Commerce 2001; Leventhal 2001).

The agreement was followed by OECD-sponsored conferences such as the symposium "Ethics in the Public Sector: Challenges and Opportunities for OECD Countries," held in Paris in November 1997; a "Workshop on Combating Corruption in Transition Economies," in Istanbul, October 1998; and the "Conference on National and International Approaches to Improve Integrity and Transparency in Government," held in Paris in July 1998. The programs were designed to reinforce the convention.

OECD, a well-funded and well-publicized antibribery program, led countries to resources they needed for addressing corruption problems and led them to whistleblowing as part of the solution. As an example, after fifteen Asian countries joined the convention on combating bribery, and signed a mutually agreed-upon initiative against corrup-tion, having been encouraged by OECD and the Asian Development Bank, they asked for assistance for developing anticorruption programs. The fifteen-nation proposal for this anticorruption assistance specifical-ly requested material on whistleblower protection (Leventhal 2001).

The U.S. Department of Commerce

Other U.S. government agencies are also heavily involved in worldwide anticorruption activities that often include promoting whistleblower protection. Especially prominent is the U.S. Department of Commerce where sections of its International Trade Administration focus exclu-sively on "good governance" in Eastern Europe, Russia, and the newly independent states. The literature and training made available to target-ed countries, with Commerce Department funding, encourage the new and developing states to grapple with whistleblower-related issues, especially citizens' fear of coming forward to expose wrongdoing (Abramov 2001).

The Department of Commerce, in cooperation with the U.S.-Russia Business Development Committee and the Russian Chamber of

Commerce and Industry, developed their own basic guidelines for appropriate business practice. The guidelines were designed as a standard or foundation for participating Russian companies to use to develop their own codes of behavior.

The issue of whistleblowing was discussed in more than one of the roundtables when the guidelines were being developed. Although the Commerce Department argued for a full disclosure policy, "disclosure" was "too foreign" a policy for the attendees and the explicit inclusion of whistleblower protection in the guidelines was opposed. However, the Russians came up with new less extreme language and the guidelines they helped develop do provide guarantees for "confidential counseling" (Abramov 2001).

Since 1996, Novgorod, Russia, has been the site of the project's pilot program. Novgorod companies used the guidelines as the basis for developing their own business ethics codes. Novgorod participants continue to be supported in that effort. In July 1999, an OECD ethics conference held in Novgorod attracted nincty participants, including Russian federal and regional officials, private-sector executives, and NGOs. Trainings continue to raise the whistleblower issue as a topic in roundtables and conferences.

While the Department of Commerce would have liked to have retained in these business guidelines a provision guaranteeing some form of protection for those who expose corruption, whistleblower protection was a principle not easily adopted there. Any new ethics code had to be fashioned to fit the cultural context, otherwise it would not work. Given the particular history and experience of the newly independent countries, it was not always possible to include protecting whistleblowers as a feature of the code (Abramov 2001).

The Importance of Culture

The former Soviet states' political history and social context influenced their receptivity to using whistleblowing as an anticorruption tool. For example, in Russia and other parts of the former Soviet Union, the concept of whistleblowing has a strong negative connotation of "snitch," not the more positive connotation of serving the public interest.[5]

However, while words themselves are charged, sometimes just finding a new phrase can help in the process of cultural change. In Novgorod, for example, the phrase "confidential counseling" seemed acceptable but "disclosure" seemed threatening and foreign. Some countries have their own special phrases to refer to their "whistle-blowers." In the Netherlands, for example, they are called "bell ringers, after those who ring church bells when danger threatens a community." Other places call them "lighthouse keepers" because their "beacon exposes rocks and danger spots that could sink ships" (Devine 2001c).

When GAP returned to Slovakia to lead a two-day workshop on whistleblowing in October 2001, they were actively engaged in "defusing" the whistleblower concept (Leventhal 2001). The Russian participants with whom they were working feared that a policy of protecting whistleblowers would revive a "culture of informants" (the old Soviet-style system). GAP made advances in dealing with their challenge by changing the term *whistleblower* to *bell ringer.*

Similarly, when the nonprofit organization Ethics Resource Center (ERC) worked with St. Petersburg businesses to create codes of ethics, they found that the term *hotlines* for reporting wrongdoing had too many negative connotations in Russia and so they had to substitute the term *helpline.* In fact, ERC also found that the term *reporting* itself (i.e., *reporting wrongdoing*) had negative connotations that prevented the Russians from using it in their ethics codes (Raven 2001).

U.S. money and good intentions were not enough, however. To be effective, anticorruption work had to be approached with enormous cultural sensitivity. For that reason, the Ethics Resource Center was tapped for the Department of Commerce's foreign anticorruption outreach efforts.

The Ethics Resource Center
and the Department of Commerce

The Ethics Resource Center, based in Washington, D.C., is a nonprofit organization that works closely with the U.S. Department of Commerce and with NGOs around the world, primarily to combat domestic corruption and to create a more stable and honest business environment.

ERC has provided assistance in a wide range of countries, including the United Arab Emirates, South Africa, Colombia, Russia, Turkey, and Mexico. The organization's activities primarily concern ethics in the business community and although whistleblowing is not the primary focus of their work, encouraging people to come forward to expose ethical wrongdoing is fundamental to their work's success (Raven 2001).

The Ethics Resource Center was originally called American Viewpoint when it was established in 1922. Its responsibilities were to teach "American values" to immigrants on Ellis Island and elsewhere. By the mid-1970s, the organization had shifted its focus to the broader areas of organizational ethics and the transmission of values.

U.S. Defense Department scandals on contract overcharges in the 1970s and 1980s created opportunities for ERC to work with businesses to establish ethical standards (Raven 2001). But the real challenges came when ERC began to work with foreign business and government leaders and with multinational corporations and their subsidiaries.

The U.S. Department of Commerce is among the sponsors that have supported ERC's international efforts. Global Integrity Exchange, an ERC initiative, periodically organizes meetings to bring together ethics and anticorruption scholars and professionals with "select representatives" from around the world. The experts offer appropriate training, mentoring, and knowledge exchange to use in the development and implementation of ethics initiatives in their private and public sectors (Ethics Resource Center 2001).

Participants from Russia and the newly independent states were able to attend ERC-initiated meetings because the U.S. Department of Commerce's Russia and Independent States Division program financially sponsored their participation. The list of the U.S. and multinational corporations that supported the work of the meetings, by being models and mentors to these Eastern European businesses, include Fannie Mae, Lockheed Martin, and American Express, among others.[6]

Starting in 1998, ERC worked with the NGO Transparency International to create ERC chapters in Colombia and South Africa (Ethics Resource Center 2001). The initial catalyst to create the ERC Ethics Center in Turkey was the multinational drug company Merck Sharp & Dohme, which was selling products there.

Merck's CEO wanted to turn its own "ethical standards" into a competitive advantage. It used the Ethics Resource Center to help it make changes in the business practices of its own Turkish subsidiary. The impulse spread. By October 2000, an Ethics Summit 2000 conference attracted three hundred Turkish business leaders and government officials (Raven 2001; Ethics Resource Center 2001).

Change would not come quickly. ERC estimated that the transformation in values of private-sector and government organizations would take a decade. But ERC also believed that with new ethics standards, people would be expected to exercise individual responsibility and they would be coming forward as whistleblowers to expose wrongdoing (Raven 2001).

The St. Petersburg project offered a similar challenge and illustrated the same general dynamic. Having connected with the Ethics Resource Center at an international conference, a group of Russian businesspeople called on ERC for assistance in creating a new organizational culture that was local, independent, and self-sustaining.

The stimulus for change came from 120 local businesses that got together and announced their "Declaration of Integrity." The companies resolved "to be committed to fair practice in business, declaring to repudiate corruption and to implement a code of business ethics as part of . . . [their] policy of corporate governance." Eventually, the St. Petersburg Center for Business Ethics was established and training, investments, and collaboration began a long process toward new codes of conduct (Ethics Resource Center 2001).

Like Turkey, a more ethical business culture in Moscow would require that individuals exercise personal responsibility and be able to blow the whistle on wrongdoing. But because of the cultural context, ERC believed that they would first have to work with the businesses to slowly build a new organizational culture. The new culture would have to include a level of trust that would encourage whistleblowers to come forward. This would require cultural sensitivity and patience. Encouraging whistleblowing was a fundamental part of their mission, they said (Raven 2001).

The American Bar Association

Also active and involved in the United States' global anticorruption reach is the American Bar Association (ABA). The ABA had always had a section on international law and practice. In the early 1990s, with the fall of communism, the Central and Eastern European Law Initiative (CEELI) was created because of interest on the part of some ABA members.

For a decade, providing support for anticorruption efforts has been a major goal for ABA-CEELI. ABA has established CEELI programs in twenty-three countries, such as Albania, Uzbekistan, and Romania. Over fifty long-term resident U.S. volunteer lawyers support these programs, assisted by over a hundred nationals in their local offices and thirty ABA staff members in Washington, D.C. Because ABA-CEELI has made anticorruption, accountability, and transparency a priority for their work, the resources they distribute include materials on whistleblower protection (Leventhal 2001).

In addition, as part of its mission, CEELI has encouraged its resident representatives to offer assistance in implementing measures that include whistleblower protection. For example, as earlier described, they worked with GAP on such a project in Slovakia. CEELI resident staff help draft new laws, train prosecutors and judges, create law libraries, and create environmental-advocacy NGOs.

Following the CEELI model in Eastern Europe, in 2000 the ABA created "analogous bodies" to cover other parts of the world, forming the African Law Initiative Council, the Latin American Law Initiative Council, and the Asia Law Initiative Council (Leventhal 2001). Their Asia Law Initiative Council was created as a result of the fifteen-nation solicitation for anticorruption programs described earlier.

International Organizations

Highly visible international organizations, similarly motivated by anticorruption campaigns, have also become involved with whistleblower rights. They have worked with U.S. organizations and have shared their goals and projects.

As the International Monetary Fund began to document the negative effects of corruption on the growth, investment, and government spending of countries around the world (Mauro 2000), the German-based watchdog organization Transparency International (TI) was polling businesspeople, politicians, and academics to calculate an index of corruption in forty-one countries, which was soon expanded to a ninety-nine-country "corruption perception index" (Crossette 1995: E-3; Transparency International 1999).

Transparency International

Transparency International is an important part of the anticorruption network. They support U.S. efforts and they promote the creation of whistleblower hotlines. If the public does not trust government officials to receive the complaints, they reason, then neutral nonprofit organizations can assist by providing hotline services to the agency. TI has even suggested a guideline such a hotline service should follow:

How do complainants expect to be treated?

When people complain they want six essential things:
    to be heard
    to be understood
    to be respected
    an explanation
    an apology, and
    remedial action as soon as possible. (Transparency International 2000)

No international group articulates more clearly how essential an ingredient whistleblowing is to good governance and anticorruption measures in newly independent countries. TI offers this guiding principle:

> For . . . measures to be effective, it is important that arrangements which allow employees to "blow the whistle" or to "ring the bell" clearly express the underlying purpose—which is to enable an individual to raise a concern so that those in authority are able to investigate it. *Unless this fundamental principle of accountability underpins the design of the system, it is unreasonable to expect it to signal—let alone deliver—a change from a culture where people are discouraged from raising the alarm.* (Transparency International 2000: chapter 25)

Other international organizations, such as the World Bank, concerned with the effects of corruption in an interdependent world, encourage whistleblowing as an anticorruption tool.

The World Bank

The International Bank for Reconstruction, commonly called the World Bank, has as its mission global financial stability and "an open international trading system." With a membership of over 170 countries, it uses loans to stimulate economic development (Lawson 2002: chapter 14).

In September 1996, James D. Wolfensohn, then president of the World Bank, committed the bank to fighting "the cancer of corruption." Following his commitment, the World Bank undertook over six hundred anticorruption programs and initiatives in ninety-five borrower countries (World Bank Group 2000)

In October 1998, as part of its anticorruption strategy, the World Bank Group established a twenty-four-hour international telephone hotline to report fraudulent or corrupt practices either in the bank or connected with contracts financed by the bank. They also established an ethics helpline used to provide ethics advice to bank staff (McCormick 2002).

The World Bank AlertLine (hotline) is maintained by an outside group, Pinkerton Consulting and Investigations. They report having received 469 calls during the period from October 1998 to January 2002; fewer than half were anonymous; almost half alleged fraud (AlertLine World Bank 2002). The World Bank posts on their web site a list of the dozens of firms and individuals who are temporarily or permanently ineligible to be awarded a World Bank finance contract because they violated fraud and corruption provisions (World Bank Group 2001).

Asian Development Bank

Another international organization, one that has a regional reach, the Asian Development Bank (ADB) adopted an anticorruption policy in 1998. The following year, the ADB established procedural guidelines for investigating and sanctioning firms and individuals engaged in corrupt practices. ADB also established a whistleblower line to their Anticorruption Unit, via telephone, fax, and e-mail. As of December 31, 1999, they had processed fifty-five cases and had disqualified ten firms and fourteen individuals from participating in ADB-financed projects because they had engaged in corrupt or fraudulent activities (Asian Development Bank 2000).

Currently, many international organizations are encouraging whistleblowing as an anticorruption tool. There have been a number of international conventions and agreements that include whistleblower-protection provisions. The OAS Inter-American Convention Against Corruption and the OECD Guidelines (already described), the Johannesburg Principles, and the European Union Civil and Criminal Law Conventions on Corruption are good illustrations (Clark 2001).

The Immigration and Naturalization Service

A recent Immigration and Naturalization Service (INS) case represents another development related to whistleblowing that potentially has wide implications outside U.S. borders. The political-asylum case, originally heard by INS, was appealed to the Ninth Circuit Court. By the terms of the 2000 court decision, for the first time, the INS would be required to treat seriously whistleblower claims for political asylum.

The U.S. Immigration and Naturalization Service offers political asylum to immigrants who demonstrate that they have been persecuted on account of political opinion. The category of political opinion was recognized by the INS to not just be limited to activities related to political parties. The INS has included political opinion that is related to trade-union activities; they have also recognized feminism as political opinion. However, in 2000, for the first time, the court also defined whistleblowing against corrupt government officials as political opinion for which asylum could be granted. In doing so, they overturned an INS decision and broke with past patterns of interpretation.

Two 1997 prior decisions, described in an Expedited Removal Study (Musalo, Gibson, and Taylor 1999: 84, 89), were typical of what had been the INS perspective on whistleblowing. Whistleblowers did not meet the INS standard for granting asylum.

One case concerns a Brazilian asylum seeker, "Ms. J.," whose husband worked in a factory where employees were involved in drug-trafficking activities. The civilians and military police were also involved in the activity. The husband told co-workers he didn't want to continue in the activity and the wife told her father who contacted the local police, which led to the arrest of the drug-trafficking perpetrators. As a result of the exposure, the couple's lives were threatened. Ms. J. sought political asylum in the United States.

On April 11, 1997, Ms. J. had her "credible fear interview" with the INS. The asylum officer found that she had not met any of the standards for granting asylum, one of which was affiliation with a political party. In addition, the INS pointed to the fact that she and her husband had initially been involved in illegal activities, and that the INS was presuming that not all Brazilian police were corrupt, and that she could relocate to another part of Brazil.

The second case concerned an Ecuadorian asylum seeker. "Mr. K." was an elected counselor of the court of second instance, responsible for the appropriation of public money for an Ecuadorian municipality. He was a member of the Social Christian Party. At a weekly meeting of elected counselors, he discovered that a large quantity of money was missing. In October 1996, Mr. K. reported the loss to the comptroller. Mr. K. accused a counselor, who was a member of another party, of embezzling the money. As a consequence, he received threats on his life.

On June 19, 1997, Mr. K. had a "credible fear interview" with the INS. They concluded that Mr. K. had not established a credible fear of persecution. They characterized the situation as a personal vendetta and said he failed to establish that the government was unwilling to protect him, and the INS presumed that location to another part of Ecuador was possible. These cases represent the generally unsympathetic response the INS gave to whistleblowers who sought political asylum.

The Grava Case

In 2000, the case of Dionesio Calunsag Grava would become the vehicle for establishing a precedent and offering a new interpretation of whistleblowing. Grava had come from the Philippines in 1991 as a non-immigrant visitor authorized to stay for only one year in the United States. Soon after, he applied to the INS for political asylum claiming persecution because he was a whistleblower. In 1994, the Immigration and Naturalization Service denied his request for asylum; his request was appealed and denied by an immigration judge in 1996, and again denied on appeal by the Board of Immigration Appeals.

In his application for political asylum, Grava provided detailed evidence for his claim. As a customs officer and a policeman, he said, he provoked persecution because of his efforts to uncover "entrenched government corruption by his supervisors." But his application was unlike others seeking asylum. They had claimed that a particular party had persecuted them, while Grava claimed he had suffered and had been persecuted from "all sides: Marcos Loyalists, Communist insurgents in the New People's Army and the Philippine military and police force" (California Daily Opinion Service 2000: 1823). The details of his story supported his claim of persecution.

In 1977, as a lieutenant in the police force working for the Philippine Bureau of Customs in the port of Mactan, he uncovered a smuggling ring involving his supervisor. As a result of blowing the whistle, Grava was retaliated against by his supervisor and was transferred to another site.

The accusations made against Grava were later cleared, and in 1987 he was eventually reassigned back to Mactan. Once again, Grava blew the whistle on smuggling activities. He exposed corruption by his new supervisor, a man who had family connections to the Philippine Congress and the National Bureau of Investigation. Grava's charges were not immediately investigated and instead, Grava was transferred to an outlying post.

In 1990, for a third time, Grava exposed "smuggling activities involving his supervisor" and once again he was transferred away from the site. When authorities did investigate his accusations, Grava came forward as a whistleblower and was able to testify, against his supervisor's orders, and prove his case. The publicity from the local press covering the case portrayed Grava as a crusader against corruption.

As a consequence of the press coverage, Grava received threats by phone, death threats by mail, his car tires were slashed, and his pet dog and monkey were poisoned. The threats were real; one of his fellow customs officers had already been killed, allegedly by the same corrupt supervisor. Grava and his family fled to the United States, where he sought asylum.

Grava testified in support of his application for asylum on August 19, 1996. His petition was reviewed and his case decided on by an Immigration and Naturalization Service Board on February 11, 2000, in Pasadena, California. The INS denied him asylum. His application was rejected, according to the record, "because it did not show that the persecution suffered was *on account of political opinion*. Instead, the Board concluded that it was a matter of personal retaliation" [italics added by author] (California Daily Opinion Service 2000: 1823). Grava appealed the decision.

In *Dionesio Calunsag Grava, Petitioner, v. Immigration and Naturalization Service, Respondent*, the Ninth Circuit Court of Appeals reversed the INS decision. They disagreed with the board's contention that whistleblowing does not constitute an expression of political opinion. They also disagreed with the conclusion that Grava failed to establish a nexus between his political opinion and his fear of persecution. Quite the contrary, they found the facts of the case and case precedent supported the presence of such a nexus.

The court was not suggesting that all whistleblowers would be granted asylum. It admitted that, legally, whistleblowing against a supervisor at work is not always "an exercise of political opinion" and that if retaliation is "completely untethered to a governmental system" it "does not afford a basis for asylum." However, "where the whistle blows against corrupt government officials," the court said, "it may constitute political activity sufficient to form the basis of persecution on account of political opinion" (p. 1824).

The court pointed to earlier cases decided in the Ninth and Seventh Circuit Courts of Appeal. These earlier cases (1) established that political agitation against corruption might be grounds for asylum, and (2) established that refusing to accede to government corruption can itself represent "political opinion" for purposes of refugee status.

In further arguing that Grava's persecution was political and a "protected activity," the court took care to point out that what Grava feared was not the "usual job hazards of a law enforcement officer." If this had been so, the dangers he faced would arise solely from the duties of his job and he could not claim political persecution. But in Grava's case, the "alleged tormentors" were "instruments of the government itself," the court said. Thus, Grava's actions were directed toward a governing institution—not merely against individuals—and Grava's persecution was political. As the court stated, "when the alleged corruption is inextricably intertwined with government operation, the exposure and prosecution of such an abuse of public trust is necessarily political" (p. 1824).

Not all foreign whistleblowers who experienced retaliation would be able to flee their countries and expect to be granted political asylum in the United States. But whistleblowers who exposed the systemic corruption of their governments (not just corruption of individuals) and could show that they feared real retaliation, could make such claims and, based on this case, might succeed. Could this ruling have the effect of encouraging whistleblowing in other countries? Perhaps in the distant future but not in the next few years, according to Hastings Law School professor Karen Musalo.

Given the overall trends in asylum law, the Grava case seems "exceptional." The interpretive trend "weighs away from the case's conclusion." In addition, the Ninth Circuit Court of Appeals is generally innovative and has a more expansive view of the rules; their interpretation is not at all reflective of the general thinking in the INS or the more conservative perspectives of the other courtrooms. Furthermore, once you get into a more "nontraditional opinion," other claims based on the same rule are "very susceptible to being denied almost mechanically" (Musalo 2001a).

Two INS cases in 2001 showed how demanding the Grava requirements would be as an asylum standard for others. There may have been whistleblower cases other than these two, but it is "close to impossible" to trace the decisions of INS asylum officers and immigration judges, according to Musalo.

In the case of Marlene Silva, submitted June 11, 2001, and decided June 27, 2001, she was found ineligible for asylum because her fear of future persecution was based on her marriage and, using the Grava rule, the INS panel asserted that fear of purely personal retribution was not a cognizable basis for asylum (*Silva-Toro* 2001).[7]

In the case of Victor Vasquez and Maria Irma Vasquez, submitted

August 8, 2001, and decided August 22, 2001, the INS panel also rejected applications for asylum. Although Victor Vasquez had exposed wrongdoing, he had secretly informed the military of illegal activities, which included blowing the whistle on the local mayor's drug trafficking. However, the INS panel reasoned that the future persecution he alleged would occur was most likely personal. Vasquez failed to show, the panel said, that "the mayor wished to persecute him on account of his actual or imputed political opinion" (*Vasquez* 2001).

The events of September 11, 2001, will certainly affect the INS decisions on asylum as well. The terrorists who attacked the twin towers of the World Trade Center in New York City and the Pentagon headquarters across the Potomac River from Washington, D.C., had entered the United States easily. There seems to be a national mood of unease and distrust of foreigners and there is no mainstream enthusiasm for encouraging or increasing immigration (*Jim Lehrer NewsHour* 2002). For this reason, it is unlikely that the INS will want to use or be encouraged to use new reasons to grant political asylum to foreigners in the near future.

Tying It All Altogether

Down the road, the Grava case might stimulate whistleblowing in other countries. After all, it elevated whistleblowing to the kind of legitimate political expression that could be rewarded with political asylum in the United States.

However, the Grava decision would have to be applied more positively, more visibly, and more often to send a forceful message that U.S. policies, even border policies, respect the dignity and legitimacy of whistleblowers. Such a message, if publicized, might actually encourage foreign nationals to risk and dare to blow the whistle on corruption. And as we have seen, the United States, in other ways, is already sending a message promoting whistleblowing to other countries.

During the last decade, the U.S. government, as well as for-profit and nonprofit organizations, have encouraged whistleblowing around the world. For most of the agencies involved, whistleblowing was not their primary goal; it was a means to an end. The ends sought were increased democracy and reduced corruption.

If the organization's primary goal was to support democracy, then encouraging whistleblowing would be a step toward that goal. The support of moral action and of individual rights, and the exercise of individual responsibility, were essential ingredients for creating more democratic countries.

If the organization's goal was to reduce corruption, then encouraging whistleblowing and developing whistleblower protection and working hotlines (or help lines), not only in the countries themselves but also in the lending agencies such as the World Bank, could help reduce corruption. Whistleblower protection would start to crack a systemic problem and could begin to address corruption in the most meaningful way possible, from the inside.

Different agents were motivated by different goals but they joined together, and whistleblowing was part of the package. The irony of a partnership that connected GAP with government and corporate interest should not be lost. GAP, which for decades had vigorously criticized government and business for not offering adequate whistleblower protection and for not respecting whistleblower rights, was now working on the same side as the State Department, the Department of Commerce, and multinational corporations. GAP had not changed. The world had changed. What GAP had always advocated—respect for individual rights and responsibilities—was now being seen as a necessary component of democracy. Gap's mantra, "whistleblower protection," was now being embraced as an anticorruption tool.

U.S. organizations and government agencies joined with a wide array of international and other-nation organizations. It needed to be a truly global effort, as Igor Abramov, from the Department of Commerce, suggested at an OECD meeting. "The need for integrity in the private sector, the fight against corruption and the promotion of good governance and transparency," he said, "have now become a global concern and an integral component to the development of democratic institutions and open economic systems around the world" (Abramov 1999). And in fact there was a dramatic convergence of forces to spread the word on foreign shores about good governance, about fighting corruption, and about the virtues of whistleblowing and the benefits of individuals acting responsibly.

The web of international activity was remarkable. Conferences and workshops were taking place everywhere. Commercial interests worked with ethicists; businesses worked with government agents and NGOs. Take USAID as an example. USAID regional bureaus worked with OECD to co-sponsor anticorruption workshops in Argentina, Turkey, and in the Philippines, with the goal of broadening the discussion of the

OECD antibribery convention. USAID also provided financial support to Transparency International that helped them establish over ninety separate TI chapters around the world.

The Ethics Resource Center projects also provide examples of international cooperation and networking. ERC work was not only funded by the U.S. Department of Commerce but their projects also often attracted World Bank funds and support from Transparency International.

Today, there are many government agencies, nonprofit organizations, and businesses of all sizes whose activities aim at addressing corruption, enhancing democracy, and creating transparency in business. But their ultimate goal is actually even more ambitious—to change the culture and practices of companies, cities, and countries. Whistleblowing is an essential part of their mission.

Notes

1. Israel was the first country to explicitly copy U.S. whistleblower protection legislation. It did not seem to happen as a result of U.S. design or effort. According to Chaim Kalchheim, from Bar-Ilan University in Israel, the Israeli whistleblower protection law was enacted as a private bill by M. K. Amnon Rubinstein, who was reportedly "inspired" by the U.S. 1978 Civil Service Reform Act providing whistleblower protection to U.S. federal government workers. On May 27, 1981, Israel's parliament, the Knesset, enacted the law that gave to Israel's public complaints commissioner the responsibility of protecting whistleblowers. The commissioner would have the right to investigate employee complaints of retaliation as a result of the employee exposing corruption in their agency, as long as the complaint was reported in "good faith."

2. For example, "The Third International Jerusalem Conference on Ethics in the Public Service: Politics, Ethics and the Professions," Jerusalem, Israel, June 25–29, 1995; "The Fifth International Conference, 'Public Sector Ethics—Between Past and Future,'" Brisbane, Queensland, Australia, August 5–9, 1996; "The Ninth International Anti-Corruption Conference," Durban, South Africa, October 1999.

3. Nations that sent visitors to GAP during this period included: Angola, Antigua, Argentina, Belize, Brazil, Bhutan, Bolivia, Canada, Chile, Costa Rica, El Salvador, France, Germany, Guatemala, Honduras, Israel, Italy, Kenya, Korea, Latvia, Macedonia, Malawi, Mexico, Mozambique, Nepal, Netherlands, Nicaragua, Nigeria, Norway, Pakistan, the Palestinian Authority, Peru, Romania, Russia, Saudi Arabia, Senegal, Serbia-Montenegro, Slovakia, South Africa, Sri Lanka, Thailand, United Kingdom, Uganda, and Vietnam.

4. Public Concern at Work is an English NGO founded in 1993 "in response to a series of scandals and disasters in the '80s and '90s" in Great

Britain. In every case of disaster, according to the organization, workers who knew of the dangers did not come forward, or if they did, they were ineffective or their company was unresponsive. Public Concern at Work came into existence to advise potential whistleblowers and expanded to offer technical assistance in whistleblowing in the UK and in other countries. The full description of the organization is available at: www.pcaw.co.uk/about/.

5. Throughout much of the twentieth century, according to Jasmine Martirossian, the word that comes closest to whistleblowing in the Russian language is *donos* or *donoschik*, which mean "the act of informing" and "informant." *Donos* was encouraged by the Soviet government as a way of controlling citizens; the practice of informing was especially widespread during the period of Stalinist repression.

6. The conferees' participation in the program has included visits to national ethics offices and discussions with distinguished ethics professionals within the for-profit, nonprofit, and governmental sectors. It also included on-site visits to major corporations. Organizations participating in this aspect of the training program have included: American Express, Citicorp, Coudert Brothers, the Defense Industry Initiative, Eastern Medical Systems, the Ethics Officer Association, Fannie Mae Corporation, International Business Ethics Institute, Lockheed Martin Corporation, the Organization for Economic Cooperation and Development, Pinkerton Services Group, the Prudential Insurance Company of America, Transparency International–USA, the United States Office of Government Ethics, the United States Sentencing Commission, United Technologies Corporation, Verizon Communications, and the World Bank Group.

7. Although the Marlene Silva case cites the Grava case, the available facts of *Silva-Toro* do not clearly show that whistleblowing was the issue. But it may have been. This case and the Vasquez case, which also cites *Grava,* were "ports of entry" cases. In "ports of entry" cases, an immigration officer hears the case, and if asylum is sought, the case is then heard by an asylum officer (AO), usually in a detention center. The AO decides if the immigrant has a "credible fear." A hearing by an immigration judge might be a possible next step, but in both these cases a hearing was denied.

Appendix:
Federal Laws
with Whistleblower Provisions

T he following is the most comprehensive list available of laws other than the Whistleblower Protection Acts that contain whistleblower-protection provisions. The list is based on materials in Daniel P. Westman's *Whistleblowing: The Law of Retaliatory Discharge* (1991); Stephen M. Kohn's *Concepts and Procedures in Whistleblower Law* (2001); Government Accountability Project, "Federal Whistleblower Laws and Related Statutes" (2001b); and Terance D. Miethe's *Whistleblowing at Work: Choices in Exposing Fraud, Waste, and Abuse on the Job* (1999).

29 USC S623(d)	Age Discrimination in Employment Act of 1997 (ADEA) (1988)
42 USC S12203	Americans with Disabilities Act of 1990 (ADA)
15 USC S2651	Asbestos Hazard Emergency Response Act (AHERA) (1986)
20 USC S3608	Asbestos School Hazard Detection and Control Act (1980)
42 USC S2000e	Civil Rights Act of 1964
10 USC S1587	Civilian Employees of the Armed Forces (1983)
42 USC S7622	Clean Air Act (1988)
42 USC S9610	Comprehensive Environmental Response, Compensation and Liability Act, CERCLA (Superfund) of 1980 (1988)
10 USC S2409	Contractor Employees of the Armed Forces (Department of Defense Authorization Act of 1984 & 1987) (1988)

29 USC S1140	Employee Retirement Income Security Act of 1974
42 USC S5851	Energy Reorganization Act of 1974 (ERA) (1978)
29 USC S206	Equal Pay Act of 1963
29 USC S215	Fair Labor Standards Act of 1938 (FLSA)
31 USC S3730(h)	False Claims Act Amendments Act of 1986
29 USC S2615	Family and Medical Leave Act of 1993 (FMLA)
41 USC S265	Federal Acquisition Streamlining Act of 1994
12 USC S1790b	Federal Credit Union Act (FCUA) (1934)
12 USC S1831j	Federal Deposit Insurance Corporation Act (1933)
12 USC S1441a	Federal Home Loan Bank Act (FHLBA) (1932)
30 USC S815(c)	Federal Mine Safety and Health Act of 1977 (FMSHA) (1988)
45 USC S441	Federal Railroad Safety Act of 1970 (FRSA)
33 USC S1367	Federal Water Pollution Control Act of 1972 (1988)
22 USC S3905	Foreign Service Act of 1980
42 USC S9610	Hazardous Substances Release Act (1988)
29 USC S1574g	Job Training and Partnership Act (JTPA) (1982)
5 USC S7211	Lloyd-LaFollette Act (1912)
33 USC S948(a)	Longshoreman's and Harbor Worker's Compensation Act (LHWCA) (1988)
18 USC S1031	Major Fraud Act of 1989 (MFA)
29 USC S1855	Migrant and Seasonal Agricultural Worker Protection Act (1988)
10 USC S1034	Military Whistleblower Protection Act (1988)
29 USC S158(a)(4)	National Labor Relations Act (Labor Relations Act) (NLRA) (Wagner-Connery Labor Relations Act) (1935)
29 USC S660(c)	Occupational Safety and Health Act of 1970 (OSHA)
38 USC S1964(c)	Racketeer Influenced and Corrupt Organizations Act (RICO) (1970)
45 USC S151	Railway Labor Act (RLA) (1926)
29 USC S703	The Rehabilitation Act of 1973
46 USC S1501	International Safe Container Act title VII 1988 (amended by the Civil Rights Act of 1991)
42 USC S300j-9	Safe Drinking Water Act (1978)
42 USC S6971	Solid Waste Disposal Act (1988)

30 USC S1293	Surface Mining Control and Reclamation Act of 1977
49 USC S2305	Surface Transportation Assistance Act of 1978 (STAA)
15 USC S2622	Toxic Substances Control Act of 1984
49 USC S42121	Wendell H. Ford Aviation and Investment Reform Act for the 21st Century (2000)

Acronyms

ABA	American Bar Association
ADB	Asian Development Bank
CEELI	Central and Eastern European Law Initiative
DCASMA	Defense Contract Administration Services Management Area
DoD	Department of Defense
DoJ	Department of Justice
DoL	Department of Labor
EPA	Environmental Protection Agency
ERC	Ethics Resource Center
FDA	Food and Drug Administration
GAO	General Accounting Office
GAP	Government Accountability Project
GSA	General Service Administration
HHS	U.S. Department of Health and Human Services
INS	U.S. Immigration and Naturalization Service
OAS	Organization of American States
OCR	Office for Civil Rights
OECD	Organization for Economic Cooperation and Development
OIG	Office of the Inspector General
INS	Immigration and Naturalization Service
MSPB	Merit Systems Protection Board
NASA	National Aeronautics and Space Administration
NRC	Nuclear Regulatory Commission
OCR	Office for Civil Rights
OSC	Office of Special Counsel

RCRA	Resource Conservation and Recovery Act
TI	Transparency International
USAID	United States Agency for International Development

Bibliography

Aberbach, Joel D. 1979. "Changes in Congressional Oversight," *American Behavioral Scientist* 22 (May-June): 493–515.

Abramov, Igor. 1999. "Commerce's Abramov Remarks to OECD Meeting on Corruption." To the Second Annual Meeting of the OECD Anti-Corruption Network for Transitional Economies. Istanbul, Turkey. 3 November. From the U.S. Department of Commerce web site (21 December 2001): www.mac.doc.gov/INTERNET/corruption.htm.

———. 2001. Senior Adviser for Eastern Europe, Russia, and Independent States, U.S. Department of Commerce, International Trade Administration. Interview by the author, 11 December.

Abramson, Jill. 1986. "Reagan Agency Pushed to the Max," *Legal Times* 9 (4 August): 1, 14–16.

———. 2002. "In This Scandal Powerful Women Play Starring Roles," *San Francisco Chronicle*, 27 January, p. A-14.

Adams, Floyd C. 1986a. Letter to Al Martinez, Chief, Civil Rights Bureau, California Department of Social Services from Floyd Adams, Director, Investigative Division, Office for Civil Rights, Region IX, 6 February.

———. 1986b. Memo to Internal Coordinator for AIDS and ARC Complaints and Inquiries from Floyd Adams, Acting Regional Manager, OCR IX, 28 February.

AlertLine World Bank. 2002. *Management Information Report for the Period 10/1/1998 to 1/31/2002.*

Alford, C. Fred. 2001. *Whistleblowers' Broken Lives and Organizational Power.* Ithaca, N.Y.: Cornell University Press.

American Bar Association. 2001. Central and Eastern European Law Initiative. From American Bar Association web site (18 December): www.abanet.org/ceeli/home.html.

Anonymous. 1989. Some of the interviews related to Hal Freeman's resignation were conducted by the author under a grant of anonymity.

Anonymous. 2001. Interview related to whistleblower Cindy Ossias was conducted by the author under a grant of anonymity, 15 February.

Apodaca, Virginia. 1986. Memo to All Staff from Virginia Apodaca, Regional Manager, OCR IX, 9 July.

———. 1989. Regional Manager, Office for Civil Rights, U.S. Department of Health and Human Services, Region IX. Interview by the author, 13 February.

Aronson, Geoffrey. 1992. "Buying Silence," *The Progressive* (August): 24–27.

Asian Development Bank. 2000. *Anticorruption Unit.* From Asian Development Bank web site (April): www.adb.org/Anticorruption/unit. asp.

Associated Press. 2001. "IRS Criticized '97 Whistleblower," *Kansas City Star*, 18 April, p. A-8.

Bailey, Stephen. 1988. "Ethics in the Public Service." In *Public Administration: Concepts and Cases,* 4th ed., edited by Richard Stillman. Boston: Houghton Mifflin.

Barnes, Robert, and JoAnne Frankfurt. 1987. "Gene Arline's Battle with Tuberculosis and Her School Board," *Access to Employment* (spring): 5–8.

Bayon, Ricardo. 2002. "Time for Financial Democracy—and Trust," *San Francisco Chronicle*, 7 February, p. A-27.

Bellone, Carl J., and George Frederick Goerl. 1992. "Reconciling Public Entrepreneurship and Democracy," *Public Administration Review* 52 (March-April): 130–134.

Bergman, Lowell. 2000. Recorded presentation, The Commonwealth Club, San Francisco, 6 January.

Berthelsen, Christian, and Scott Winokur. 2001. "Power Juggling Ramped Up Price," *San Francisco Chronicle*, 20 May, pp. A-1, 21.

Berube, Bertrand. 1988. "We Need a Whistle-Blower Protection Act," *Washington Post,* 30 July, p. A-22.

Boffey, Philip. 1986. "NASA Had Warning of a Disaster Risk Posed by Booster," *New York Times*, 7 February, pp. 1, 32.

Boisjoly, Roger. 2001a. Morton Thiokol (NASA) Whistleblower. Interview by the author, 23 March.

———. 2001b. Interview by the author. 3 October.

———. 2001c. Unpublished presentations, University of San Francisco, 3 October.

Boisjoly, Russell P., Ellen Foster Curtis, and Eugene Mellican. 1989. "Roger Boisjoly and the Challenger Disaster: The Ethical Dimensions," *Journal of Business Ethics* 8 (the Netherlands) (1989): 217–230.

Bok, Sissela. 1981. "Blowing the Whistle." In *Public Duties: The Moral Obligations of Government Officials*, edited by Joel L. Fleishman, Lance Liebman, and Mark H. Moore. Cambridge, Mass.: Harvard University Press.

Bollier, David. 2002. "Let the Information Flow." From web site (30 April): http://www.nader.org/history/bollier_chapter_4.html.

Bonner, Raymond. 1983a. "E.P.A. Officials Say Inquiry Data Have Been Erased or Are Missing," *New York Times*, 20 February, p. 1.

———. 1983b. "EPA Administrator Said to Ask Inquiries on Miss Lavelle's Actions," *New York Times*, 21 February, p. 14.

Bowman, Ann O. 1988. "Superfund Implementation: Five Years and How Many Changes." In *Dimensions of Hazardous Waste Politics and Policy*, edited by Charles E. Davis and James P. Lester. Westport, Conn.: Greenwood Press.

Bowman, James S., Frederick A. Elliston, and Paula Lockhart. 1984. *Professional Dissent: An Annotated Bibliography and Research Guide*. New York: Garland.

Branch, Taylor. 1979. "Courage Without Esteem: Profiles in Whistle-Blowing." In *Culture of Bureaucracy*, edited by Charles Peters and Michael Nelson. New York: Holt, Rinehart, and Winston.

Bunting, Glenn F. 1985. "Navy Whistle-Blower to Testify Before House Panel," *Los Angeles Times*, 30 September, pp. 3, 10.

Burke, John P. 1986. *Bureaucratic Responsibility*. Baltimore: Johns Hopkins University Press.

Burnham, David. 1982a. "Paper Chase of a Whistle-Blower," *New York Times*, 16 October, p. 9.

———. 1982b. "Environmental Unit Accused of Seeking to Silence a Critic," *New York Times*, 11 December, p. 11.

———. 1983. "Tension Bubbles in the Bureaucracy: E.P.A. Shakeup Is Rooted in Clash of Appointees and Civil Servants," *New York Times*, 13 March, sec. 4, p. 2.

California Daily Opinion Service. 2000. *Dionesio Calunsag Grava, Petitioner v. Immigration and Naturalization Service, Respondent*. No. 98–70981 United States Court of Appeals for the Ninth Circuit; INS No. A70–186–394. *The Recorder*. 8 March (also found at 00 C.D.O.S. 1823).

California State Assembly Committee on Insurance. 2000. *Final Report on Department of Insurance Enforcement Practices and Priorities*. (Reproduced by the state assembly.)

Camus, Albert. 1969. *The Fall*. New York: Alfred A. Knopf.

Chaddock, Gail Russell. 2002. "Enron Changes Climate for Whistle-Blowers," *Christian Science Monitor*, 1 March, p. 5.

Chalk, Rosemary, and Frank von Hippel. 1979. "Due Process for Dissenting 'Whistle-Blowers,'" *Technology Review* 81 (June-July): 49–55.

Cheney, Dick, Secretary of Defense. 1989. *Defense Hotline Program*. A memorandum prepared for the secretaries of the military departments, 22 May.

Christiansen, Jon P. 1975. "A Remedy for the Discharge of Professional Employees Who Refuse to Perform Unethical or Illegal Acts: A Proposal in Aid of Professional Ethics," *Vanderbilt Law Review* 28: 805–841.

Chronicle Sacramento Bureau. 2000. "Lawyer Who Leaked Audits Reinstated at State Agency," *San Francisco Chronicle*, 30 November, p. A-7.

Cimons, Marlene. 1986. "U.S. Rights Aid Charges a Bias, Quits," *Los Angeles Times*, 22 February, p. 4.

Cinnamond, William G. 1989. Director of Legislative and Public Affairs, Office of Special Counsel. Interview by the author, 4 August.

Clark, Louis. 1978. "The Sound of Professional Suicide," *Barrister* 5 (summer): 10–13, 19.

————. 1986. "Blowing the Whistle on Public Health and Safety Dangers and Environmental Hazards," Government Accountability Project, 16 May.

————. 1988. "A Year of Victories Amidst Steadily Expanding Need. Government Accountability Project Annual Report for July 1987–June 1988." 7 September, unpublished report.

————. 2001. Letter to Alexander Wilde. Ford Foundation, 1 May.

————. 2002. Executive Director of the Government Accountability Project. Interview by the author, 4 May.

Cook, Tim. 1987. "Courts Rule on 504 Employment Coverage," *Mainstream* (May): 15, 17–19.

Cooper, Melvin G. 1979. "Administering Ethics Laws: The Alabama Experience," *National Civic Review* 68 (February): 77–81, 110.

Cooper, Terry. 1984. "Public Administration in an Age of Scarcity: A Citizenship Role for Public Administration." In *Politics and Administration,* edited by Jack Rabin and James S. Bowman. New York: Marcel Dekker.

Cranston, Alan. 1986. Letter to Otis Bowen, Secretary of Health and Human Services, 26 February.

Crossette, Barbara. 1995. "A Global Gauge of Greased Palms," *New York Times,* 20 August, p. E-3.

D'Antonio, Michael. 1993. *Atomic Harvest: Hanford and the Lethal Toll of America's Nuclear Arsenal.* New York: Crown Publishers.

Davidson, Joe. 1986. "HHS Aide Is Said to Receive $87,000 of U.S.-Paid Trips," *Wall Street Journal,* 7 August, p. 30.

Davies, J. Clarence. 1984. "Environmental Institutions and the Reagan Administration." In *Environmental Policy in the 1980s,* edited by Norman Vig and Michael Kraft. Washington, D.C.: CQ Press.

Davis, Joseph. 1983. "Burford Resigns from EPA; Congress Gets Documents." *Congressional Quarterly Weekly Report,* 12 March, pp. 495–498.

DeLeon, Peter. 1993. *Thinking About Political Corruption.* Armonk, N.Y.: M. E. Sharpe.

Department of Commerce. 2001. *OECD Guidelines: Rule of Law for Business and Anti-Corruption Initiatives.* From U.S. Department of Commerce Market Access and Compliance web sites (21 December): www.oecd.org/daf/psd/acnetwork.htm and www.bisnic.doc.gov/bisnis/country/codebusen.html

Department of Commerce Inspector General. 1989. *Semiannual Report to the Congress, October 1, 1988–March 31, 1989.*

Department of Defense Inspector General. 1988–1989. *Semiannual Report to the Congress, October 1988 to March 31, 1989.*

————. 1989. *Semiannual Report to the Congress, April 1–September 30, 1989.*

————. 1992. *Semiannual Report to the Congress, April 1–September 30, 1992.*

————. 1992–1993. *Semiannual Report to the Congress, October 1992 to March 31, 1993.*

————. 1993. *Semiannual Report to the Congress, April 1–September 30, 1993.*

————. 1997. *Semiannual Report to the Congress, April 1–September 30, 1997.*

Department of Health and Human Services, Region IX. 1986. "Your Rights as a Person with AIDS or Related Conditions."

Devine, Thomas. 1988. "Whistleblowers Need Protection from Their Protectors," *Federal Times*, 20 June, editorials, pp. 9, 39.

———. 1997. *The Whistleblower's Survival Guide: Courage Without Martyrdom*. Washington D.C.: Fund for Constitutional Government, Government Accountability Project.

———. 1999. "The Whistleblower Protection Act of 1989: Foundation for the Modern Law of Employment Dissent," *Administrative Law Review* 51, no. 2 (spring).

———. 2001a. "A Report on the Anti-Corruption Conference Held in Bratislava, Slovakia, June 18–22, 2001, and Other Related Activities," Memo To: Louis Clark, Executive Director, From: Tom Devine, Legal Director, Government Accountability Project, 31 August.

———. 2001b. *Testimony to Working Group on Probity and Public Ethics, Organization of American States*. 31 March.

———. 2001c. Legal Director of the Government Accountability Project. Interview by the author, 13 August.

Devine, Thomas M., and Donald G. Aplin. 1986. "Abuse of Authority: The Office of the Special Counsel and Whistleblower Protection," *Antioch Law Journal* 4 (summer): 5–71.

Devine, Thomas, and Jeff Ruch. 1993. *Government Accountability Project, Testimony Before the House Committee on Post Office and Civil Service Subcommittee on Civil Service on Oversight of the Whistleblower Protection Act*. 31 March.

Devine, Thomas, and Frank Morales. 2001. Comments to the *Consultative to the Document: Raising Concerns About Serious Wrongdoing*, Proposed Amendments to the European Union Staff Regulations. Government Accountability Project, 31 March.

Diaz, Tom. 1983. "'Whistleblowers' Hard to Sort Out," *Washington Times*, 1 November. Quoted in Senate 1983: Hearings Before the Subcommittee on Administrative Practice and Procedure of the Committee on the Judiciary, *Examining the Role of Whistleblowers in the Administrative Process*, 98th Cong., 1st Sess., 14 November, p. 157.

Dilulio, John J., Jr., Gerald Garvey, and Donald F. Kettl. 1993. *Improving Government Performance: An Owner's Manual*. Washington, D.C.: Brookings Institution.

Dirks, Raymond L., and Leonard Gross. 1974. *The Great Wall Street Scandal*. New York: McGraw Hill.

Dotson, Betty Lou. 1986. Memo to Regional Managers from Betty Lou Dotson, Acting Deputy Director, Office of Program Operations, Health and Human Services, 12 February.

Dowd, Maureen. 1983. "Superfund, Supermess," *Time*, 21 February, pp. 14–16.

———. 2002. "Barbie Loves Math," *New York Times*, 6 February, p. A-21.

Dymally, Mervyn M. 1986a. Letter to Henry A. Waxman, Chair, Subcommittee on Health and the Environment, 10 March.

———. 1986b. Letter to Ted Weiss, Chair, Intergovernmental Relations and Human Resources Subcommittee, 10 March.

Early, Pete. 1984. "Top Pentagon Auditors Win Merit Board Fight," *Washington Post*, 26 July, p. A-19.

Egan, Thomas E. 1990. "Wrongful Discharge and Federal Preemption: Nuclear Whistleblower Protection Under State Law and Section 210 of the Energy Reorganization Act," *Boston College Environmental Affairs Law Review* 17 (winter): 405–440.

Ellis, Virginia. 2001. "Bill Proposes Protections for State Lawyers," *Los Angeles Times*, 22 February, p. A-3.

Ellis, Virginia, and Rone Tempest. 2000. "Funds Went to Host of Non-Quake Purposes; Insurance: Records Show That Research Foundation Set Up by Quackenbush Gave Hundreds of Thousands to Athletic Programs and Social Service Groups. The Commissioner Defends the Expenditures," *Los Angeles Times*, 25 April, p. A-1.

Elliston, Frederick, John Kennan, Paula Lockehart, and Jan van Schaick. 1985. *Whistleblowing Research: Methodological and Moral Issues.* New York: Praeger.

"E.P.A. Check on Critic." 1982. *New York Times,* 3 July, p. 5.

Ethics Resource Center. 2001. From Ethics Resource Center web sites (9 December): www.ethics.org/international.html; www.ethics.org/southafrica.html; and www.ethics.org/colombian.html.

Ewing, David W. 1977. *Freedom Inside the Organization.* New York: E. P. Dutton.

Fairbanks, Katie. 2002. "Enron Sets Nation to Whistleblowing," *Dallas Morning News*, 27 February.

Farnsworth, Clyde H. 1988. "In Defense of the Government's Whistle Blowers," *New York Times*, 26 July, p. 10.

Fineman, Howard, and Michael Isikoff. 2002. "Lights Out: Enron's Failed Power Play," *Newsweek*, 21 January, pp. 14–24.

Fitzgerald, A. Ernest. 1972. *The High Priests of Waste.* New York: W. W. Norton.

Fletcher, George P. 1993. *Loyalty: An Essay on the Morality of Relationships.* New York: Oxford University Press.

Freeman, Hal. 1985. Memo to File Re: Complaint from Philip Monfette, 30 December.

———. 1986a. Memo to Betty Lou Dotson, Director, Office for Civil Rights, 7 February.

———. 1986b. Letter of Resignation to Betty Lou Dotson, Director, OCR, 20 February.

Frome, Michael. 1978. "Blowing the Whistle on Waste," *Center Magazine* (November-December): 50–58.

Fukumoto, James ("Jim"). 1989. Office for Civil Rights, U.S. Department of Health and Human Services Headquarters, staff. Interview by the author, 20 February.

Geiger, H. Jack. 1990. "Generation of Poison and Lies," *New York Times* 5 August, p. E-19.

General Accounting Office (GAO). 1989. "Federal Fraud Hotline Operations," *Statement of Brian P. Crowley, Director of Planning and Reporting, Accounting and Financial Management Division, Testimony Before the Subcommittee on General Services, Federalism, and the District of*

Columbia Committee on Governmental Affairs, U.S. Senate. 13 November.

———. 1992a. *Whistleblower Protection: Survey of Federal Employees on Misconduct and Protection from Reprisal,* Fact Sheet for the Chairman, Subcommittee on the Civil Service Committee on Post Office and Civil Service, House of Representatives. July.

———. 1992b. *Whistleblower Protection: Determining Whether Reprisal Occurred Remains Difficult.* Report to Chairman, Subcommittee on the Civil Service, Committee on Post Office and Civil Service, House of Representatives. October.

———. 1993. *Whistleblower Protection: Reasons for Whistleblower Complainants' Dissatisfaction Need to be Explored.* Report to Chairman, Subcommittee on the Civil Service, Committee on Post Office and Civil Service, House of Representatives. November.

———. 1999. "Nuclear Safety: Department of Energy Should Strengthen Its Enforcement Program," *Statement of Ms. Gary L. Jones, Associate Director, Energy Resources, and Science Issues, Resources, Community, and Economic Development Division, Testimony Before the Subcommittee on Oversight and Investigations, Committee on Commerce, House of Representatives.* 29 June.

Gest, Ted. 1981. "Blowing the Whistle on Waste: A Thankless Job," *U.S. News & World Report,* 29 June, pp. 50–51.

Gilman, Stuart C. 1989. "An Enemy of the People Revisited: Administrative and Ethical Dilemmas of Whistle-Blowing." Paper presented to the American Society for Public Administration, Miami, Florida, April.

Glazer, Myron Peretz, and Penina Migdal Glazer. 1988. "Individual Ethics and Organizational Morality." In *Ethics, Government, and Public Policy: A Reference Guide,* edited by James S. Bowman and Frederick A. Elliston. New York: Greenwood Press.

———. 1989. *The Whistleblowers: Exposing Corruption in Government and Industry.* New York: Basic Books.

Gledhill, Lynda. 2000. "Insurance Lawyer Gets Immunity for Hearings; She Testifies Monday—Quackenbush Aides Also Subpoenaed," *San Francisco Chronicle,* 24 June, p. A-6.

———. 2001. "Ex-Workers Say Plant Exploited Power Flow," *San Francisco Chronicle,* 23 June, pp. A-1, 11.

Goodsell, Charles T. 1994. *The Case For Bureaucracy: A Public Administration Polemic.* Chatham, N.J.: Chatham House Publishers.

Gore, Al. 1993a. *From Red Tape to Results: Creating a Government That Works Better and Costs Less: Report of the National Performance Review.* Washington, D.C.: GPO.

———. 1993b. *A Revolution in Government.* A statement by the Vice President. 3 March.

Gormley, William T., Jr. 1989. *Taming the Bureaucracy: Muscles, Prayers, and Other Strategies.* Princeton, N.J.: Princeton University Press.

Government Accountability Project (GAP). 1989a. *Fact Sheet on Major Provisions of Whistleblower Protection Act.*

————. 1989b. "Whistleblowing Hits the Big Time—Recent National Campaigns and Cases," press release, 2 February.

————. 1997. *The Whistleblower's Survival Guide: Courage Without Martyrdom.* Washington D.C.: Fund for Constitutional Government.

————. 1999. "DOE Proposes Restart of Nuclear Reactor, GAP Charges the Decision Signals Possible Preparation for Battlefield Weapons," press release, 18 August.

————. 2001a. *Blowing the Whistle on Russia's Nuclear Roulette.* From the Government Accountability Project web site (August).

————. 2001b. "Federal Whistleblower Laws and Related Statutes." Information flyer.

————. 2001c. "Watchdog Groups File Formal Notice on Lawsuit over Hanford Reactor Restart, 'Notice of Intent' Letter to Energy Dept. Cites Conflict of Interest in Environmental Study by Contractor and Failure to Address Terrorist Attack Scenario," press release, 27 September.

————. 2002a. "Bridging the Gap," newsletter (spring).

————. 2002b. "Whistleblower Rights Campaign Surges," press release, 3 May.

Graf, Michael, and Matthew Orr. 2002. "Enron's Greatest Sin," *San Francisco Chronicle*, 7 February, p. A-27.

Graff, Leonard. 1986. Letter to Hal Freeman from Leonard Graff, Legal Director, National Gay Rights Advocates, 18 February.

Graham, Jill W. 1986. "Principled Organizational Dissent: A Theoretical Essay." In *Research in Organizational Behavior,* edited by Barry Stan and L. L. Cummings. Greenwich, Conn.: Ai jai Press, 1986.

Greenfield, Meg. 1978. "Blowing the Whistle," *Newsweek*, 25 September, p. 112.

Grigg, William. 1987. "The Thalidomide Tragedy—25 Years Ago," *FDA Consumer* (February): 14–17.

Gruber, Judith E. 1987. *Controlling Bureaucracies: Dilemmas in Democratic Governance.* Berkeley: University of California Press.

Grumm, John G., and Stephen L. Wasby. 1980. "Introduction by the Symposium Coeditors," Symposium on the Analysis of Policy Impact, *Policy Studies Journal* 8 (summer): 849–851.

Hall, Charlie. 1989. Assistant Inspector General for Inspections and Resource Management, U.S. Department of Commerce. Interview by the author, 4 August.

Helmer, James B., Jr., Ann Lugbill, and Robert Clark Neff Jr. 1999. *False Claims Act: Whistleblower Litigation.* Charlottesville, Va.: Lexus Law Publishing, pp. 75, 77.

Henry, William A., III. 1982. "This Ice Queen Does Not Melt," *Time*, 18 January, pp. 16, 19.

"HHS Executive Quits in AIDS Dispute." 1986. *Oakland Tribune,* 22 February, p. 85.

"HHS Official Quits, Cites Policy on Denial of Help to Persons with AIDS." 1986. *Daily Labor Report*, 26 February, pp. A-2, 3.

"High Cost of Whistling." 1977. *Newsweek*, 14 February, pp. 75–77.

Hirschman, A. O. 1970. *Exit, Voice, and Loyalty; Responses to Decline in*

Firms, Organizations, and States. Cambridge, Mass.: Harvard University Press.

Hoffman, Pat. 1989. Office for Civil Rights U.S. Department of Health and Human Services, Headquarters, staff. Interview by the author, 17 and 20 February.

Hood, James P. 1986a. Memo to George Lyon, Acting Associate General Counsel Re: *Monfette v. San Francisco Sheriff's Department,* from James Hood, Special Assistant to the Director, Office of Program Operations, OCR/HHS, 14 February.

———. 1986b. Memo to Acting Regional Manager, OCR IX, from James Hood, Special Assistant to the Director, Office of Program Operations, 27 February.

House of Representatives. 1982. *Resource Conservation and Recovery Act Reauthorization: Hearings Before the Subcommittee on Commerce, Transportation, and Tourism of the Committee on Energy and Commerce,* 97th Cong., 2nd Sess., 31 March and 21 April.

———. 1987. Committee on Government Operations, News Release, 16 April 1987.

———. 1993. Committee on Science, Space, and Technology. *Environmental Restoration and Waste Management: Hearing Before the Subcommittee on Energy of the Committee on Science, Space, and Technology,* 103rd Cong., 1st Sess., 26 August.

Howard, John. 2000. "Insurance Department Employee Says She Was Ordered to Shred Documents," Associated Press State and Local Wire, 26 June, BC cycle.

Hyland, J. Brian. 1989. *The Inspector General's Message: U.S. Department of Labor Semiannual Report, 1 October 1988–31 March 1989.*

International Bank for Reconstruction and Development/World Bank. 1997. *World Development Report. The State in a Changing World.* New York: Oxford University Press.

Isbell, Florence. 1977. "Dissidents in the Federal Government," *Civil Liberties Review* (September-October): 72–75.

Jim Lehrer NewsHour. 2002. "Terrorism's Impact on Immigration" segment, 1 January.

Johnson, Roberta Ann. 1991. "Barbara Moulton, Early Whistleblower," *San Jose Studies* (spring): 34–43.

Johnson, Roberta Ann, and Michael E. Kraft. 1990. "Bureaucratic Whistleblowing and Policy Change," *Western Political Quarterly* 43 (December): 849–874.

Johnston, David Cay. 1999a. "Job Fears Push IRS Workers to Relax Their Effort," *New York Times,* 18 May, p. A-1.

———. 1999b. "Tax Professionals See Pitfalls in New IRS," *New York Times,* 18 July, p. 1-21.

———. 1999c. "IRS Rewards Those Who Told of Abuses," *New York Times,* 11 November, p. A-25.

———. 1999d. "Reducing Audits of the Wealthy, IRS Turns Eyes to the Working Poor," *New York Times,* 15 December, p. A-1.

————. 2000a. "IRS More Likely to Audit the Poor and Not the Rich," *New York Times,* 16 April, p. A-1.

————. 2000b. "Inquiries Find Little Abuse by Tax Agents," *New York Times,* 15 August, p. C-1.

Jonathan, Will. 1960. "The Feminine Conscience of FDA: Dr. Frances Oldham Kelsey," *Saturday Review* (September): 41–43.

Jones, Alex. 1986. "Journalists Say NASA's Reticence Forced Them to Gather Data Eleswhere," *New York Times,* 9 February, p. 30.

Jos, Philip H. 1991. "The Nature and Limits of the Whistleblower's Contribution to Administrative Responsibility," *American Review of Public Administration* 21 (June): 105–118.

Kalchheim, Chaim. 1997. "Whistleblowing in Israel: Feeling the Effects of White Corruption," Bar-Ilan University, Israel, 1997.

Kaufman, Hugh. 1989. Environmental Protection Agency whistleblower. Interviews by Michael Kraft (University of Wisconsin, Green Bay), 11 July and 1 August.

Kelsey, Frances Oldham. 1962. "Kennedy Says This About Thalidomide," *U.S. News & World Report,* 13 August, p. 14.

————. 1988. "Thalidomide Update: Regulatory Aspects," *Teratology* 38.

————. 1989. Division of Scientific Investigations, Office of Compliance, Center for Drug Evaluation and Research, Food and Drug Administration, Rockville, Maryland. Interview by the author, 13 March.

Ketab, George. 1992. *The Inner Ocean: Individualism and Democratic Culture.* Ithaca, N.Y.: Cornell University Press.

Kingdon, John W. 1995. *Agendas, Alternatives and Public Policies.* Boston: Little, Brown.

Kleinfield, N. R. 1994. "Lives of Courage and Sacrifices, Corruption and Betrayals in Blue," *New York Times,* 25 April, p. A-1.

Kmiec, Douglas W. 1988. Memorandum to Arthur B. Culvahouse Jr., counsel to the president, from Douglas W. Kmiec, acting assistant attorney general, Office of Legal Counsel.

Kohn, Stephen M. 2001. *Concepts and Procedures in Whistleblower Law.* Westport, Conn.: Quorum Books.

Kohn, Stephen M., and Michael D. Kohn. 1986. "An Overview of Federal and State Whistleblower Protections," *Antioch Law Journal* 4: 99–152.

Kraft, Michael E., and Norman J. Vig. 1984. "Environmental Policy in the Reagan Presidency," *Political Science Quarterly* 99 (fall): 415–439.

Krauss, Clifford. 1994. "Police Graft Inquiry in New York Says It Found 'Willful Blindness,'" *New York Times,* 7 July, p. A-1.

Kurtz, Howard. 1986. "HHS Aide's Travel Expense Probed," *Washington Post,* 25 September, p. A-4.

————. 1987. "HHS Civil Rights Chief Resigns Amid Probe," *Washington Post,* 12 March, p. A-17.

Kusen, Nancy. 1989. U.S. Department of Defense whistleblower. Personal statement.

Latané, Bibb, and John M. Darley. 1970. *The Unresponsive Bystander: Why Doesn't He Help?* New York: Appleton-Century Crofts.

Lawson, Kay. 2002. *The Human Polity: A Comparative Introduction to Political Science*. Boston: Houghton Mifflin.

Lazarus, David. 2001. "Whistle-Blowers Give Evidence to PUC That Prices Were Illegally Manipulated," *San Francisco Chronicle*, 19 May, pp. A-1, 11.

"Leak That Sank Rita." 1986. *Washington Monthly* (January): 18–19.

Lear, John. 1960. "Drug Makers and the Government—Who Makes the Decisions?" *Saturday Review* (New York), 2 July, pp. 37–42.

———. 1962. "The Unfinished Story of Thaliomide," *Saturday Review* (New York), 1 September, pp. 35–40.

Leventhal, Robert. 2001. Central and Eastern European Country Director, Criminal Law Reform Program, American Bar Association/Central and Eastern European Law Initiative (CEELI). Interview by the author, 20 December.

Lochhead, Carolyn. 2002. "Enron VP Testifies Executives Duped Lay," *San Francisco Chronicle*, 15 February, pp. A-1, 21.

Lochhead, Carolyn, and Zachary Coile. 2002. "House Panel Slams Firm for Shredding Enron Papers," *San Francisco Chronicle*, 25 January, pp. A-1, 24.

Los Angeles Times. 2000. "Quakenbush Whistle-Blower Exonerated," *San Francisco Chronicle*, 30 November, p. A-13.

Louis, Arthur M. 2002. "Why Auditors Weren't Likely to Blow Whistle," *San Francisco Chronicle*, 19 January 19, pp. B-1, 2.

Lucas, Greg, and Robert Salladay. 2002. "Ex-Insurance Czar Won't Face Charges," *San Francisco Chronicle*, 6 February, pp. A-17, 18.

Lynch, Jim. 1999a. "Raising Hell at Hanford," *Seattle Times,* 17 October. From the *Seattle Times* web site (August 2001): http://archives.seattletimes. nwsource.com/cgi-bin/texis/web/vortex/display?slug=pruud&date= 19991017.

———. 1999b. "The Whistle-Blower: Casey Ruud and Hanford's Hard Truths. Raising Hell at Hanford. How Bad Were the Leaking Tanks? And Did Anyone but a Couple of Whistle-Blowers Really Want to Find Out?" *Seattle Times Magazine* (17 October).

Macpherson, Mike. 1989. Hal Freeman's partner. Interview by the author, 31 January.

Maitland, Leslie. 1983. "House Unit to Get Subpoenaed Data," *New York Times*, 17 February, p. 11.

Manduna, Penuell. 1999. Invitation letter to Anti-Corruption Conference, Minister of Justice and Constitutional Developments, Durban, South Africa, 10–15 October.

Marlow, Ruth. 1986. "Civil Rights Office at HHS Described as 'Out of Control,'" *Federal Times*, 25 August, p. 7.

Martirossian, Jasmine. 1997. "Whistleblowing in Russia," unpublished paper. Northeastern University, Boston, Massachusetts.

Mason, Marcy. 1994. "The Curse of Whistle- Blowing," *Wall Street Journal*, 14 March, p. A-14.

Mathews, Jay. 1986. "HHS Worker Resigns in Protest: Regional Office Says

Help Barred in AIDS Discrimination Cases," *Washington Post*, 22 February, p. A-26.

Mauro, Paolo. 2000. "The Effects of Corruption on Growth, Investment, and Government Expenditure," from International Monetary Fund Working Paper 96/98 (September): http://www.img.org/external/pubs/ft/issues6/index.htm.

Mayer, Carolyn, and Amy Joyce. 2002. "Blowing the Whistle," *Washington Post*, 29 April, pp. H-1, 5.

McCloskey, Frank. 1993. *Statement of Chairman, Oversight Hearing on the Whistleblower Protection Act.* 103rd Cong., 1st Sess., 31 March.

McClure, Phyllis. 1986. Letter to Hal Freeman from Phyllis McClure, NAACP Legal Defense Fund, 26 March.

McCormick, John. 2002. World Bank Investigation Unit, Senior Counsel. Interview by the author, 9 January.

McCormick, Sheila. 1989. "Whistleblowers Receive Consideration on Capitol Hill," *PA Times* 12, no. 8 (2 June).

McKee, Mike. 2002. "Bar Has Guide for Whistlers," *The Recorder* (29 January): 1, 10.

McNeil, Donald G., Jr. 1979. "E.P.A. Aides Assert Disposal Rules Exempt Some Highly Toxic Rules," *New York Times*, 19 July, p. 18.

Mead, George Herbert. 1917. "Josiah Royce—A Personal Impression," *International Journal of Ethics* 27: 168–170.

Meier, Kenneth. 1985. *Regulation Politics, Bureaucracy and Economics.* New York: St. Martin's Press.

Mertzman, Robert, and Peter Madsen. 1992. *Engineering Ethics: The Case of the Challenger.* Pittsburgh: Center for the Advancement of Applied Ethics, Carnegie Mellon.

Miceli, Marcia P., and Janet P. Near. 1992. *Blowing the Whistle: The Organizational and Legal Implications for Companies and Employees.* New York: Lexington Books.

Miethe, Terance D. 1999. *Whistleblowing at Work: Tough Choices in Exposing Fraud, Waste, and Abuse on the Job.* Boulder, Colo.: Westview Press.

Mintz, Morton. 1965. *The Therapeutic Nightmare.* Boston: Houghton Mifflin.

———. 1989. *Washington Post* reporter. Interview by the author, 1 August.

Mitchell, Greg. 1979. "The Deadly Silence," *Feature* (March): 48–57.

Monfette, Philip. 1985. Complaint Alleging Discrimination Against the City and County of San Francisco, 18 December.

Morrison, Blake. 2001. "Whistle-Blowing on Rise," *USA Today*, 24–25 December, p. 1.

Moulton, Barbara. 1989. Food and Drug Administration whistleblower. Interview by the author, 3 August and 15 November.

Murphy, Kim. 2000a. "Government Finally Hears a Nuclear Town's Horrors," *Los Angeles Times*, 5 February, p. A-1.

———. 2000b. "Radioactive Waste Seeps Toward Columbia River," *Los Angeles Times*, 12 March, p. A-1.

Musalo, Karen. 2001a. Professor, Hastings College of Law. Interview with the author, 6 November.

———. 2001b. Interview with the author, 3 December.

Musalo, Karen, Lauren Gibson, and J. Edward Taylor. 1999. *Report on the Second Year of Implementation of Expedited Removal.* San Francisco: Center for Human Rights and International Justice, University of California, Hastings College of Law, Expedited Removal Study, May.

Nadel, Mark V. 1971. *The Politics of Consumer Protection.* New York: Bobbs Merrill Company.

Nader, Ralph, Peter J. Petkas, and Kate Blackwell. 1972. *Whistleblowing: The Report of the Conference on Professional Responsibility.* New York: Grossman.

Nestor, John. 1989. Food and Drug Administration staff. Interview by the author, 2 August.

Neustadt, Richard E. 1980. *Presidential Power: The Politics of Leadership from FDR to Carter.* New York: Wiley.

Newsweek. 1977. "The High Cost," 14 February, p. 75.

New York Times. 1999. "IRS Whistle-Blower Saved from the Ax," in *San Francisco Chronicle*, 17 April, p. A-3.

———. 2002."'Lone Voice': Excerpts from Testimony of Executive Who Challenged Enron," 15 February, pp. C-1, 6.

Nigro, Felix, A., and Lloyd G. Nigro. 1988. *Modern Public Administration.* 7th ed. New York: Harper and Row.

Noah, Timothy. 1989. "Shielding the Whistleblowers," *Newsweek*, 27 March, p. 32.

Noonan, John T. 1984. *Bribes.* New York: Macmillan.

Nusbaum, Marci Alboher. 2002. "Blowing the Whistle: Not for the Fainthearted," *New York Times*, 10 February, p. BU-10.

Office for Civil Rights. 1986. "Region IX Procedures for AIDS/ARC," revised in October.

Office of Special Counsel, U.S. Merit Systems Protection Board. 1988. *A Report to Congress from the Office of the Special Counsel, Fiscal Year 1987.* Washington, D.C.: U.S. Merit Systems Protection Board.

———. 2000. "U.S. Office of Special Counsel Announces Favorable Settlement of Complaints Alleging Retaliation Against Whistleblower by the Immigration and Naturalization Service," press release, 10 March.

Oneglia, Stewart B. 1986. Letter to Floyd Adams from Stewart Oneglia, Chief, Coordination and Review Section, Civil Rights Division, U.S. Department of Justice, 29 January.

Oppel, Richard A., Jr. 2002. "Ex-Chief of Enron Will Not Testify Before Congress," *New York Times*, 11 February, pp. A-1, 20.

Ossias, Cindy. 2000. "Quackenbush: Whistleblower's Tale," *Sacramento Bee*, 23 July, Forum, p. 1.

———. 2001a. California Department of Insurance whistleblower. Interview by the author, 20 February.

———. 2001b. Interview by the author, 9 March.

———. 2001c. Interview by the author, 17 December.

Parmerlee, M. A., J. P. Near, and T. C. Jensen. 1982."Correlates of Whistle-Blowers' Perception of Organizational Retaliation." *Administrative Science Quarterly* 27 (March): 17–34.

Patterson, Thomas E. 1998. *We the People.* New York: McGraw Hill.

Pear, Robert. 1986. "AIDS Victims Gain in Fight on Rights," *New York Times,* 8 June, pp. 1, 30.

Pender, Kathleen. 2002. "Stanford Dean's Role in Enron," *San Francisco Chronicle*, 7 February, pp. B-1, 3.

Perry, James L. 1989. "The Organizational Consequences of Whistleblowing," unpublished manuscript.

Peters, Charles, and Taylor Branch. 1972. *Blowing the Whistle: Dissent in the Public Interest.* New York: Praeger.

Presidential Commission on the Space Shuttle Challenger. 1986. *Report of the Presidential Commission on the Space Shuttle Challenger Accident.* Washington, D.C.: GPO, 6 June.

Public Concern at Work. 2001. From Public Concern at Work web site (20 December): www.pcaw.co.uk/about/.

Putnam, Robert D. 2002. "Bowling Together," *American Prospect* 13, no. 3. (11 February).

Quirk, Paul. 1980. "Food and Drug Administration." In *The Politics of Regulation*, edited by James Q. Wilson. New York: Basic Books.

Raloff, Janet. 1990. "Hanford's Fallout: Increased Thyroid Risks," *Science News* 138, no. 3 (21 July): 39.

Rasor, Dina. 1989. *Project on Military Procurement, Testimony Before the Senate Governmental Affairs Subcommittee on General Services, Federalism, and the District of Columbia.* 13 November.

Raven, Cherie. 2001. Consultant, International Department, Ethics Resource Center. Personal interview with author, 28 November.

Reay, Tom. 1990. Sailor stationed on the USS *Fulton*, 1986–1987. Personal interview with author, 5 April.

Rich, Spencer. 1987. "HHS Accused of Failing to Enforce Antibias Laws," *Washington Post,* 17 April, p. 20.

Richtel, Matt. 2001. "Witnesses Say Generator Cut Power Supply to Raise Price," *New York Times*, 23 June.

Robertson, Richard. 1989. AIDS Coordinator, Office for Civil Rights, U.S. Department of Health and Human Services, Region IX. Interview by the author, 16 February.

Robison, Wade L. 1994. "Trust and the Rule of Law." Paper presented at the Fourth International Conference on Ethics and the Public Service, Stockholm, Sweden, 16 June.

Royce, Josiah. 1908. *The Philosophy of Loyalty.* New York: Macmillan.

Rubin, Leon M. 2000."Alumni Profiles," *UB Today*, University of Buffalo, Buffalo, New York.

Rutland, Ginger. 2000. "Meanwhile, Back at the Office. . . ," *Sacramento Bee*, 23 July, Forum, p. 12.

Sabatier, Paul A. 1987. "Knowledge, Policy-Oriented Learning, and Political Change: An Advocacy Coalition Framework," *Knowledge: Creation, Utilization, Diffusion* 8: 649–692.

Salladay, Robert. 2000. "Attorney Tells How Insurers' Fine Was Slashed; Quackenbush Aide Told Her to Shred Papers Urging Big Levy," *San Francisco Examiner*, 26 June, p. 1.

San Francisco Weekly. 1993. vol. xii, no. 23 (4 August).

Schilts, Randy. 1986. "Civil Rights Official Quits over AIDS Policy," *San Francisco Chronicle*, 22 February, pp. A–1, 3.

Schmidt, Susan, and Peter Behr. 2002. "Lawyer Says Enron Rebuffed Concerns About Shady Deals," *Washington Post,* in *San Francisco Chronicle,* 7 February, pp. A–1, 7.

Schneider, Keith. 1994. "New Finding Raises Danger from Arms-Plant Emissions," *New York Times* 143, 22 April, p. A–21.

Sciolino, Elaine. 2001. "CIA Warms to Showbiz Limelight," *San Francisco Chronicle*, 6 May, p. A–12.

Senate. 1960. Subcommittee on Antitrust and Monopoly of the Committee on the Judiciary. *Administered Prices: Hearing Before the Subcommittee on Antitrust and Monopoly of the Committee on the Judiciary*, 86th Cong., 2nd Sess., 15 February, 17, 18 May, 1, 2, 3, and 6 June.

———. 1962a. Antitrust Subcommittee of the Committee on the Judiciary. *Drug Industry Antitrust Act: Hearings on H.R. 6245*, 87th Cong., 2nd Sess., 17, 18, 23, and 24 May.

———. 1962b. Subcommittee on Reorganization and International Organization of the Committee on Government Operations. *Interagency Coordination in Drug Research and Regulation: Hearing Before the Subcommittee on Reorganization and International Organizations of the Committee on Government Operations*, 87th Cong., 2nd Sess., 1 and 9 August.

———. 1963. Subcommittee on Reorganization and International Organizations of the Committee on Government Operations. *Interagency Coordination in Drug Research and Regulation: Hearing Before the Subcommittee on Reorganization and International Organizations of the Committee on Government Operations*, 88th Cong., 1st Sess., 20 March.

———. 1979. Subcommittee on Oversight of Government Management of the Committee on Governmental Affairs. *Oversight of Hazardous Waste Management and the Resource Conservation and Recovery Act: Hearings Before the Subcommittee on Oversight of Government Management of the Committee on Governmental Affairs,* 96th Cong., 1st Sess., 19 July and 1 August.

———. 1983. Subcommittee on Administrative Practice and Procedure of the Committee on the Judiciary. *Examining the Role of Whistleblowers in the Administrative Process: Hearings Before the Subcommittee on Administrative Practice and Procedure of the Committee on the Judiciary,* 98th Cong., 1st Sess., 14 November.

———. 1989. John N. Sturdivant, National President of American Federation of Government Employees (AFL-CIO), speaking to the Committee on Governmental Affairs Subcommittee on General Services, Federalism, and the District of Columbia, on Waste, Fraud and Abuse "Hotline" Operations, 101st Cong., 1st Sess., 13 November.

———. 1995. Committee on Energy and Natural Resources. *Hanford Nuclear Reservation: Hearing Before the Committee on Energy and Natural Resources*, 104th Cong., 1st Sess., 22 March.

————. 2002. *Congressional Record.* Testimony by Mr. Leahy (for himself, Mr. Daschle, Mr. Durbin, and Mr. Harkin) on S2010. 12 March: S1785-S1790.

Shabecoff, Philip. 1982a. "Persistent Whistle-Blower at E.P.A," *New York Times,* 14 April, p. 20.

————. 1982b. "House Charges Head of E.P.A. with Contempt," *New York Times,* 17 December, pp. 1, 20.

————. 1983. "E.P.A. and Aide Reach Settlement Averting Hearing on Harassment," *New York Times,* 15 February, p. 19.

Silva-Toro. 2001. INS No. A70–552–902. Ninth Circuit Court.

Sinton, Peter. 1997. "Whistle-Blowing Gaining Steam: Employees Have Gotten Millions for Exposing Fraud at Work," *San Francisco Chronicle,* 11 August, p. E-1.

Slovic, Paul, Baruch Fischhoff, and Sarah Lichenstein. 1979. "Rating the Risks," *Environment* 21, no. 3 (April): 14–20, 36–39.

Smith, Dan, and Patrick Hoge. 2000. "Testimony Grave for Quackenbush," *Sacramento Bee,* 27 June, p. 1.

Soeken, Karen L., and Donald R. Soeken. 1987. "A Survey of Whistleblowers: Their Stressors and Coping Strategies." Reprinted in *Whistleblowing Protection Act of 1987,* Hearings Before the Senate Subcommittee on Federal Services, Post Office and Civil Service Committee on Governmental Affairs, 100th Cong., 1st Sess., 20 and 31 July 1987.

Squatriglia, Chuck. 2001. "Probe Finds 'Artificial Shortages,'" *San Francisco Chronicle,* 18 May, pp. A-1, 17.

Stephens, Joe. 2002. "Enron Played Hardball Politics," *Palm Beach Post,* 10 February, pp. A-1, 20.

Steward, Julie, Thomas Devine, and Dina Rasor. 1989. "Courage Without Martyrdom: A Survival Guide for Whistleblowers." Washington, D.C.: Government Accountability Project and Project on Military Procurement, October.

Sturdivant, N. John. 1989. *National President, American Federation of Government Employees (AFL-CIO). Statement Before the Committee on Governmental Affairs Subcommittee on Government Services, Federalism, and the District of Columbia, U.S. Senate on Waste Fraud and Abuse "Hotline" Operations,* 13 November.

Taylor, Stuart, Jr. 1983a. "Dingell Says He Has Evidence of E.P.A. 'Criminal Conduct,'" *New York Times,* 2 March, pp. 1, 22.

————. 1983b. "E.P.A. Inquiries Center on Four Issues," *New York Times,* 13 March, p. 36.

Tedesco, Kevin. 2001. Communications Manager at CBS-TV News. Interview by the author, 13 August.

Transparency International. 1999. "A Guide to Graft," *The Economist* 353, no. 8.

————. 2000. *TI Source Book 2000.* From Transparency International web site (20 December): www.transparency.org/sourcebook/index.html.

————. 2001. *Anticorruption.* From Transparency International web site (20 December): www.transparency.org/anti-corruption/index.html.

Truelson, Judith A. 1986. "Blowing the Whistle on Systematic Corruption." Ph.D. dissertation, University of Southern California, Los Angeles.

United States Agency for International Development (USAID). 2001a. Democratization and Anticorruption Program Description. From USAID web site (27 December): www.usaid.gov/democracy/anticorruption/ usaidprogrs.html.

———. 2001b. *A Handbook on Fighting Corruption.* Anti-Corruption and Good Governance Resources. From USAID web site (28 December): www.usaid.gov/democracy/anticorruption/resources.html.

U.S. Merit Systems Protection Board, Office of Merit Systems Review and Studies. 1984. *Blowing the Whistle in the Federal Government: A Comparative Analysis of 1980 and 1983 Survey Findings,* Washington, D.C., October.

———. 1987. "Blowing the Whistle on Systematic Corruption: On Maximizing Reform or Minimizing Retaliation," *Corruption and Reform* 2 (spring): 55–74.

———. 1993. A Report to the President and the Congress of the United States by the U.S. Merit Systems Protection Board. *Whistleblowing in the Federal Government: An Update.* Washington, D.C., October.

———. 1996. *Annual Report for Fiscal Year 1995.*

Vandivier, Kermit. 1972. "The Aircraft Brake Scandal," *Harper's Magazine* (April): 45–52.

Vasquez. 2001. INS Nos. A70-797-929/A29-918-390. Ninth Circuit Court.

Vaughan, Diane. 1996. *The Challenger Launch Decision: Risky Technology, Culture, and Deviance at NASA.* Chicago: University of Chicago Press.

Vaughn, Robert G. 1999. "State of Whisleblower Statutes and the Future of Whistleblower Protection," *Administrative Law Review* 51, no. 2 (spring): 581–625.

Vig, Norman J., and Michael E. Kraft. 1984. *Environmental Policy in the 1980s: Reagan's New Agenda.* Washington, D.C.: CQ Press.

Vogel, L. Robert. 1991. "Deterrent Effects of 'Whistleblower' Lawsuits Justify False Claims Act," *Aviation Week & Space Technology* (4 November): 73–74.

Wade, Beth. 1998. "At the Hot End of the Cold War," *The American City & County* 113, no. 3 (Pittsburgh) (March): 20–30.

Wakefield, Susan. 1976. "Ethics and Public Service: A Case of Individual Responsibility." *Public Administration Review* 36 (November-December): 661–666.

Wald, L. Matthew. 1998. "Admitting Error at a Weapons Plant; Belatedly, Energy Department Deals with Leaks of Nuclear Waste," *New York Times,* 23 March, p. A-10.

———. 2000. "Questioning Whistle-Blower's 'Delusions': Labor Department Faults Utility's Psychiatric Exam of Nuclear Worker," *New York Times,* 11 April, p. A-21.

Washington Monthly. 1986. "The Leak That Sank Rita," (January): 18–19.

Weisband, Edward, and Thomas M. Franck. 1975. *Resignation in Protest.* New York: Grossman.

Westin, Alan, ed. 1981. *Whistle-Blowing: Loyalty and Dissent in the Corporation.* New York, McGraw Hill.

Westman, Daniel P. 1991. *Whistleblowing: The Law of Retaliatory Discharge.* Washington, D.C.: Bureau of National Affairs.

White House. 1993. *The National Performance Review.* 3 March.

Whitlock, Stephen A. 1989. Assistant Inspector General for Special Programs, U.S. Department of Defense. Interview by the author, 3 August.

Wilson, James Q. 1989. *Bureaucracy: What Government Agencies Do and Why They Do It.* New York: Basic Books.

Wilson, James Q. (ed.). 1980. *The Politics of Regulation.* New York: Basic Books.

Wood, B. Dan. 1988. "Principals, Bureaucrats, and Responsiveness in Clean Air Enforcements," *American Political Science Review* 82: 213–234.

World Bank Group. 2000. "The World Bank Fights Corruption," fact sheets from the World Bank web site (April): http://worldbank.org/html/extdr/pb/pbcorruption.htm.

———. 2001. "Procurement Policy: World Bank Listing of Ineligible Firms. Fraud and Corruption," from the World Bank web site (July 2002): http:www.worldbank.org/html/opr/procure/debarr.html.

———. 2002. "Anticorruption," from the World Bank web site (July 2002): http:www.worldbank.org/publicsector/anticorrupt/.

Yardley, Jim. 2002. "Ex-Enron Official's Apparent Suicide," *San Francisco Chronicle,* 26 January, pp. A-1, 15.

Zuckerman, Sam. 1998. "Pat the Giant Killer," *San Francisco Chronicle,* 14 November, p. D-1.

Index

About the Book

Whistleblowers can ruin lives—and save them. Is it worth it? Roberta Ann Johnson explores when and how—and to what effect—people make the choice to blow the whistle. Engrossing case studies from the tobacco industry, to NASA, to the FDA illustrate clearly how individual efforts can and do transform institutions, shape public policy, and serve as a force for democratization.

Roberta Ann Johnson is a professor of politics at the University of San Francisco.